THE 1916 IRISH REBELLION

THE 1916 IRISH REBELLION

Bríona Nic Dhiarmada

Foreword by Mary McAleese

University of Notre Dame Press   Notre Dame, Indiana

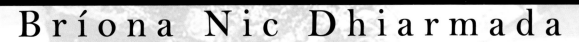

First published in the United States in 2016 by
Universty of Notre Dame Press
Notre Dame, Indiana 46556
undpress.nd.edu

First published in Ireland by
Cork University Press
Cork, Ireland

Printed in Canada by Friesens Corporation

Library of Congress Cataloging-in-Publication Data

Names: Nic Dhiarmada, Bríona, author.
Title: The 1916 Irish Rebellion / Bríona Nic Dhiarmada ; foreword by
Mary McAleese.
Description: Notre Dame, Indiana : University of Notre Dame Press, 2016. |
Includes bibliographical references and index.
Identifiers: LCCN 2015042508 | ISBN 9780268036140 (hardcover : alk. paper) |
ISBN 0268036144 (hardcover : alk. paper)
Subjects: LCSH: Ireland—History—Easter Rising, 1916. | Irish question.
Classification: LCC DA962 .N53 2016 | DDC 941.5082/1—dc23
LC record available at http://lccn.loc.gov/2015042508

∞ *This paper meets the requirements of ANSI/NISO Z39.48-1992 (Permanence of Paper).*

Contents

Joseph McGill, *Church Street Barricades, 1916.*

Foreword

As we mark the centenary of the dramatic events of the 1916 Easter Rising, a generation that is shaped by it but also removed from it by time and tides dares to both commemorate and reflect deeply on the received narratives, perceptions, and attitudes gifted to us by the past. This book, and the documentary series to which it is a companion volume, takes on the task of closely reexamining and reevaluating important aspects the story of 1916 and in particular its locus within the British imperial project.

A work of many years of scholarship, it is an initiative of the Keough-Naughton Institute for Irish Studies at the University of Notre Dame. It is an attempt to go beyond what has long been a strictly insular approach to Irish history usually concentrating on the contested relationship between Ireland and Britain. Instead, this book places the Irish Rising in its European and global contexts and traces the impact of the Rising as anticolonialism found its voice in the wake of the First World War. It tells the story of how an apparent defeat turned into an epoch-defining event of world history. The 1916 uprising started a ripple that would spread far beyond the shores of Ireland. It would lead to an independent Irish state and help to change the map of the world, marking the beginning of the end of the British Empire. It would also affect Irish America in a profound way. The book explores the crucial role of the United States and of Irish America in both the lead-up to and the aftermath of the events in Dublin. The importance of the "American Connection" as it relates to the Easter Rising would be hard to exaggerate. For example, the *New York Times* carried page 1 stories on the events in Dublin for fourteen consecutive days from April 25 to May 8, 1916, relegating stories of the carnage of World War One to the sidebars and inside pages.

The 1916 Irish Rebellion presents this pivotal historical event, with its global significance, to a broad audience in a highly accessible manner that is both serious and informative but also highly visual and evocative in its use of photographs and personal testimony. The 1916 Irish Rising was not only an event with historical and current ramifications, it is also a story of real men and women, people of flesh and blood who participated in or witnessed epoch-making events, with many leaving firsthand accounts of their experiences. These personal accounts are presented separately from the central narrative, allowing us to hear these voices from the past directly. They are the voices of those who were there. This is history at its most intimate. These very human stories are not always given their due place in the telling of that history, but they are listened to here. They are at the heart of the 1916 Rising and at the heart of this book. I hope that through these stories we can look with fresh eyes and insight at the contested historical issues, bringing them to a broad audience in a way that fosters a deeper historical, cultural, and human understanding.

MARY MCALEESE
(President of Ireland, 1997–2011)
November 2015

Preface

Five years ago the University of Notre Dame's Keough-Naughton Institute for Irish Studies, led by its director and by Professor Bríona Nic Dhiarmada, made a decision to explore the 1916 Easter Uprising in all its historic dimensions. We were struck by how American filmmaker Ken Burns had managed to take exhaustive and cutting-edge research on the U.S. Civil War and make it accessible to millions of viewers worldwide. We wondered if we could do something similar for the 1916 Dublin rebellion. This led to years of research in libraries and film archives worldwide, to wide consultation with historians and experts in multiple countries, to the assembly of a first-rate creative and production team in Ireland and the United States, to filming in seven countries, and finally to a landmark three-part documentary for worldwide public television, narrated by Liam Neeson, and this book.

The Easter 1916 Uprising was a brief event in a small country with long-term consequences for the world in which we live. It is an Irish story. It is an English story. It is an American story. It is a World War I story. Most profoundly, it is a deeply human story.

I take this opportunity to thank everyone involved with the project who shared our dream but especially Keough-Naughton Institute Faculty Fellow and Thomas J. and Kathleen M. O'Donnell Professor of Irish Studies Bríona Nic Dhiarmada, who oversaw every aspect of the 1916 project and who wrote the script and this book.

CHRISTOPHER FOX
Professor and Director of the Keough-Naughton Institute for Irish Studies
September 2015

PART ONE

Awakening

DUBLIN, JUNE 11, 2011

TWO WOMEN, BOTH SOVEREIGN HEADS OF state, came together in an historic moment. One hundred years had passed since the last visit of a British monarch to Dublin. Queen Elizabeth of the United Kingdom of Great Britain and Northern Ireland and Mary McAleese, President of Ireland, stood in the Garden of Remembrance in Parnell Square. This memorial garden is dedicated to "all those who gave their lives in the cause of Irish free-dom." Prominent among those are the men and women of the Easter Rebellion of 1916. Here, on the same spot where the defeated rebels were held before being marched off, some to prison, some to their deaths before British firing squads, Queen Elizabeth bowed her head and laid a wreath in memory of her erstwhile enemies. It was a remark-able moment in the long and turbulent history of these two neighboring islands.

President Mary McAleese with Queen Elizabeth at the Garden of Remembrance, Dublin, June 11, 2011.

Dublin, July 8, 1911

THE PAST, LITERALLY ANOTHER COUNTRY: Dublin was still second city of the British Empire. Thousands of people were on the streets to greet the newly crowned King George V shortly after his accession to the British throne. Led by a squadron of the 8th Royal Hussars, the royal party made their way with much pageantry and ceremony from Kingstown Harbor, as it was then

Crowds line the streets at College Green, Dublin, 1911, to greet the newly crowned King George V.

known, to Dublin Castle in the center of the city, the grey stone fortress begun by King John in 1204. The royal visit attracted much coverage in the Irish and British press and was hailed as an unmitigated triumph.

On leaving Dublin Castle, George V's message to his Irish subjects spoke of his gratitude for "the spontaneous and hearty loyalty that has greatly touched our hearts." He looked forward to "coming amongst our Irish people again, and at no distant date."

George V was not to get his wish to return to his Irish subjects. Although it could hardly be imagined at the time, his was to be the last visit of a reigning British monarch to Dublin for one hundred years. It would soon become apparent that the carefully choreographed show of loyalty merely papered over the fault lines that continued to exist between these two neighboring islands and within Ireland itself. The decade following George V's visit would see armed insurrection, political upheaval, and remarkable changes that would turn previous arrangements on their head and help change the map of the world forever.

King George V, 1911.

Half the great fog of misunderstanding and suspicion that has brooded so long over the relations between England and Ireland has been cleared away in the seven mile roar of welcome.
—*Daily Telegraph*,
July 10, 1911

There has been no royal progress in Ireland in our memory witnessed by such mammoth crowds as those of Saturday, and no British sovereign coming to our shores has had such a reception as that accorded our royal visitors on Saturday. The Royal Progress into the heart of our capital proved regal and glittering even beyond dreams.
—*Irish Independent*,
July 10, 1911

The Age of Empire

THE EARLY YEARS OF THE TWENTIETH century were the heyday of empire. By the end of the nineteenth century, the British Empire had become the greatest in the world. It was the empire on which the sun never set. By the beginning of the new millennium, "Her Majesty Victoria," as her official title had it, "by the Grace of God, of the United Kingdom of Great Britain and Ireland, Queen, Defender of the Faith, Empress of India," ruled over 14 million square miles and over 450 million people. It seemed that the age of empire would never end as Western powers scrambled over each other to acquire further colonies. The spirit of imperialism was the order of the day.

The White Man's Burden

Take up the White Man's burden—
Send forth the best ye breed—
Go bind your sons to exile
To serve your captives' need;
To wait in heavy harness,
On fluttered folk and wild—
Your new-caught, sullen peoples,
Half-devil and half-child.

Take up the White Man's burden—
In patience to abide,
To veil the threat of terror
And check the show of pride;
By open speech and simple,
An hundred times made plain
To seek another's profit,
And work another's gain.

Take up the White Man's burden—
The savage wars of peace—
Fill full the mouth of Famine
And bid the sickness cease;
And when your goal is nearest
The end for others sought,
Watch sloth and heathen Folly
Bring all your hopes to nought.

Take up the White Man's burden—
No tawdry rule of kings,
But toil of serf and sweeper—
The tale of common things.
The ports ye shall not enter,
The roads ye shall not tread,
Go mark them with your living,
And mark them with your dead.

Take up the White Man's burden—
And reap his old reward:
The blame of those ye better,
The hate of those ye guard—
The cry of hosts ye humour
(Ah, slowly!) toward the light:—
"Why brought he us from bondage,
Our loved Egyptian night?"

Take up the White Man's burden—
Ye dare not stoop to less—
Nor call too loud on Freedom
To cloke your weariness;
By all ye cry or whisper,
By all ye leave or do,
The silent, sullen peoples
Shall weigh your gods and you.

Take up the White Man's burden—
Have done with childish days—
The lightly proffered laurel,
The easy, ungrudged praise.
Comes now, to search your manhood
Through all the thankless years
Cold, edged with dear-bought wisdom,
The judgment of your peers!

—Rudyard Kipling[1]

Map showing British Empire, 1886.

Queen Victoria.

opposite: Queen Victoria's jubilee procession in London, 1897.

"That Most Distressful Country"

As the new century turned, Britain and the other imperial powers continued to acquire new territories in parts of the world. But Britain's oldest, and indeed most troublesome, conquest was much closer to home. For Britain, Ireland remained unfinished business. For Ireland and the Irish, the British Empire was seen as a mixed blessing, and the attitude of the Irish to it remained ambivalent.

England had attempted to control and pacify Ireland since the Norman invasion in the twelfth century. King John began building Dublin Castle in 1204, and it acted both symbolically and literally as the bulwark of English rule in Ireland over the next seven hundred years. The area around Dublin was known as the Pale and demarcated the boundary of English influence and rule in Ireland. England gradually strengthened its control of Ireland. From the Tudor period onward, plantation was a central plank in attempts to subdue the rebellious Irish. Religion became a marker of difference between the native Irish and the conquering English, now added to those of culture, language, and ethnicity. During the fifteenth and sixteenth centuries, England became a Protestant country, whereas the Irish remained resolutely Catholic. A sequence of plantations continued during the sixteenth and seventeenth centuries during which the land of Catholic rebels was confiscated and given to English Protestant settlers, often as a reward for military service. The plantation of Ulster in the seventeenth century saw over half a million acres change hands and would establish a sizeable population of Protestants in the province. Throughout Ireland, power and land were now concentrated in the hands of a new Protestant elite. This ruling elite would be known as the Ascendancy.

For the next three hundred years, the vast majority of Protestants would see themselves as the king's men, provided that the king was Protestant. They considered themselves distinct from the dispossessed Irish Catholics, who were considered disloyal and therefore not to be trusted. This English consolidation was marked by regular outbreaks of rebellion by the Irish. The mass of Catholic Irish would remain outside the Pale for many years to come. This was to have complicated and enduring consequences both for Anglo-Irish relations and within Ireland itself. Following the failed rebellion of the United Irishmen of 1798, when both Catholic and Protestant radicals united

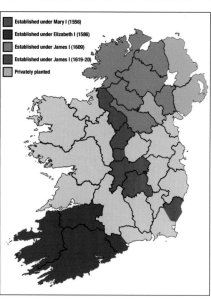

Maps showing Ireland before and after the plantations of the sixteenth and seventeenth centuries.

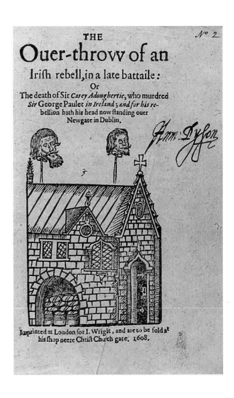

in armed insurrection against English rule, Ireland lost its parliament and under the provisions of the Act of Union of 1800 became an integral part of the United Kingdom of Great Britain and Ireland. Those who supported the Union were known henceforth as unionists.

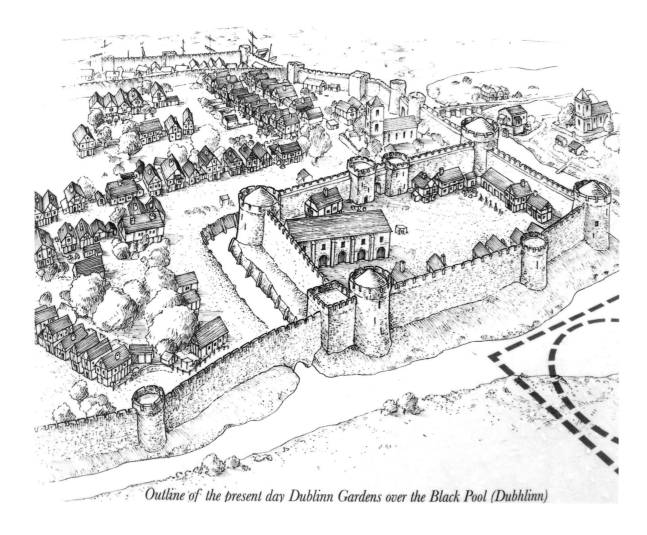

Outline of the present day Dublinn Gardens over the Black Pool (Dubhlinn)

The latter years of Victoria's reign saw a succession of imperial processions throughout the empire. In 1900 Victoria visited Ireland, and over fifty thousand Dubliners, waving Union Jacks, gathered in the Phoenix Park to greet her.

As the citizens of Dublin cheered Queen Victoria, just as they had during her jubilee celebrations three years earlier, it appeared that following centuries of conflict—punctuated by rebellions from the Gaelic chieftains to the Rebellion of 1798 and the most recent Fenian uprising—the "Irish Question" was close to resolution and Ireland was settling into her role within the empire. Not all the queen's subjects were equally enamored, however.

Artist's impression of Dublin Castle, bulwark of English rule in Ireland.

Despite the overt show of support for the empire on the streets of Dublin, these years had also seen an upsurge in national feeling expressed through what was primarily, initially at least, a cultural revolution. Beyond the apparent dormancy of Irish resistance, nationalist sentiment, both political and cultural, was beginning to stir. By the time of Victoria's visit, a new generation was beginning to make its voice heard. That voice, although still very much in the minority, would become in the next decade increasingly loud and more anti-imperial in its expression of animus. Some of that animus was clearly expressed even as Queen Victoria was receiving her loyal subjects in Dublin. To the radicals and republicans who protested at her visit, she was still "The Famine Queen." Maud Gonne, a leading figure in radical separatist circles, did not mince words: "The visit of the Queen of England is a political action, and if we accord her a welcome we shall stand shamed before the nations. The world will no longer believe in the sincerity of our demand for national freedom."

One of the primary reasons for Victoria's visit to Dublin was to help in the recruitment of the Irish into the British Army, which was then locked in a bitter struggle on the veldts and plains

left: Queen Victoria visiting Dublin, 1900,

right: A young Maud Gonne.

of the Transvaal in South Africa, where Afrikaner farmers and miners waged a guerrilla war against the British. In the war's first year, the British had suffered heavy casualties. The Boer War would last from 1899 to 1902 and have a profound impact on opinion in Ireland. With Irishmen fighting on both sides of the conflict and with both opponents and supporters active on the home front, it would rehearse many of the fault lines that ran and would continue to run through Irish history.

Twelve different Irish regiments fought with the British in South Africa. Many rank-and-file soldiers who "took the queen or king's shilling" joined not from any pro-imperial sentiment but from economic necessity. They were recruited mostly in the slum areas of the major cities. Other regiments, such as the Munster Fusiliers, recruited from Cork City as well as from rural areas in Kerry and other counties. In addition to the regular army battalions, three companies of the Thirteenth Battalion Imperial Yeomanry were raised in Ireland, one in Dublin and two in Belfast. They were drawn from the highest echelons of those who supported the Union with Britain, unionist and Ascendancy families, ready once again to show their loyalty to queen and, later, king and country.

opposite: Boer fighters, 1900.

Munster Fusiliers during the Boer War.

Other Irishmen, however, fought on the other side, with the Boers, inspired by their common enmity to Britain. The Irish contingent comprised two commando units, the first time this word was used in modern warfare. The first, the Irish Transvaal Brigade, was composed of Irish and Irish American miners living and working in the mines of the Transvaal prior to the war. They were joined by a group of volunteers from Chicago and other volunteers who came from America and Ireland to fight against the British. Among them was a young nationalist and separatist from County Mayo named John McBride. As Major McBride, he took command of the Irish Transvaal Brigade and carved out a reputation for himself as a brave and resourceful commander.

Overall about thirty thousand Irishmen fought in the Boer War on the side of the British. Some five hundred fought for the Boers. During the course of the war, one thousand Irishmen on both sides lost their lives and were buried on the veldt. At the end of the war and the defeat of the Boers, a triumphal arch was erected in St Stephen's Green in honor of the Royal Dublin Fusiliers and their contribution to the war effort. Known officially as Fusiliers' Arch, it became known to nationalists as "Traitors Gate."

The Boer War was highly significant in galvanizing the vast majority of Irish nationalists in their support of the Boers. Here was a "small nation" standing up to the British Empire and being suppressed with an unrelenting ferocity. Photographs of Boer women and children behind the barbed wire of internment camps inflamed Irish nationalist opinion, as they did liberal opinion within Britain itself.

In Ireland the anti-war movement, known initially as the Irish Transvaal Committee, brought together people from differing factions and strands of radical thought, literary figures, Gaelic Leaguers, cultural activists, radical separatists, suffragettes, and feminists, as well as followers of the nascent labor and socialist movements. Many of the individuals who would became important activists and leaders in 1916 cut their political teeth during this period. They learned how to organize, how to agitate, how to propagandize. They would become the backbone of the revolutionary intelligentsia.

above: Major John McBride.

opposite: Boer women and children in a concentration camp.

New Beginnings

Since the 1880s a renaissance in national sentiment had burgeoned as new organizations brought fresh energy to what seemed a moribund culture. Douglas Hyde's essay "The Necessity for De-Anglicising Ireland" acted as a call to arms. The Irish language, a new national theater and national literature, as well as Gaelic games became central to this renaissance. Figures such as Hyde himself, W. B. Yeats, Lady Gregory, A.E. (George William Russell), and individuals who would become prominent revolutionaries, such as Pádraig Pearse, engaged in a mining and recuperation of the Irish past. Many figures in this new Irish Revival were drawn from the ranks of the Protestant Ascendancy, following in the steps of previous Protestant radicals such as Theobald Wolfe Tone and Thomas Davis, who had spearheaded the growth of republican and nationalist ideas in the eighteenth and nineteenth centuries.

This newly motivated sense of national identity owed much to an invigorated sense of cultural nationalism, which could be seen through a variety of organizations that became prominent in the 1880s, such as Conradh na Gaeilge, also known as the Gaelic League, an Irish language revival movement; the Gaelic Athletic Association (GAA), which sought to promote indigenous Irish games in opposition to the imperial games of cricket and soccer; as well as the more general Irish Literary Revival, which put forward the idea of a uniquely Irish national literature. Although many in the forefront of these movements were drawn from the Protestant Ascendancy class, many of the rank and file were drawn from the newly urbanized Catholic middle and lower middle classes as well as from the ranks of an increasingly militant organized labor movement. Another movement of note within nationalism was Sinn Féin (We Ourselves), a small political party founded by journalist Arthur Griffith in 1905. His book *The Resurrection of Hungary: A Parallel for Ireland* advocated a dual monarchy for Ireland, as had occurred in Austro-Hungary, and caused much debate in nationalist circles.

Dublin, indeed Ireland, was a small place. People such as Arthur Griffith, Maud Gonne, Helena Moloney, James Connolly, Countess Markievicz, Pádraig Pearse, and Thomas MacDonagh increasingly moved in similar circles with various stands of radicalism cross-fertilizing the others. Women increasingly were being politicized in Ireland and Britain through the suffrage movement. Maud Gonne, a scion of an Ascendancy family, "a society girl," was not only a feminist and

A young Douglas Hyde.

Lady Gregory.

Joseph Mary Plunkett.

William Butler Yeats.

Pádraig Pearse.

To say that Ireland has not prospered under English rule is simply a truism; all the world admits it, England does not deny it. But the English retort is ready. You have not prospered, they say, because you would not settle down contentedly, like the Scotch, and form part of the Empire. 'Twenty years of good, resolute, grandfatherly government', said a well-known Englishman, will solve the Irish question. He possibly made the period too short, but let us suppose this. Let us suppose for a moment—which is impossible— that there were to arise a series of Cromwells in England for the space of one hundred years, able administrators of the Empire, careful rulers of Ireland, developing to the utmost our national resources, whilst they unremittingly stamped out every spark of national feeling, making Ireland a land of wealth and factories, whilst they extinguished every thought and every idea that was Irish, and left us, at last, after a hundred years of good government, fat, wealthy, and populous, but with all our characteristics gone, with every external that at present differentiates us from the English lost or dropped; all our Irish names of places and people turned into English names; the Irish language completely extinct; the O's and the Macs dropped; our Irish intonation changed, as far as possible by English schoolmasters into something English; our history no longer remembered or taught; the names of our rebels and martyrs blotted out; our battlefields and traditions forgotten; the fact that we were not of Saxon origin dropped out of sight and memory, and let me now put the question—How many Irishmen are there who would purchase material prosperity at such a price? . . .

In conclusion, I would earnestly appeal to every one, whether Unionist or Nationalist, who wishes to see the Irish nation produce its best— surely whatever our politics are we all wish that—to set his face against this constant running to England for our books, literature, music, games, fashions, and ideas. I appeal to every one whatever his politics—for this is no political matter—to do his best to help the Irish race to develop in future upon Irish lines, even at the risk of encouraging national aspirations, because upon Irish lines alone can the Irish race once more become what it was of yore—one of the most original, artistic, literary, and charming peoples of Europe.

—Douglas Hyde, "The Necessity for De-Anglicising Ireland"[3]

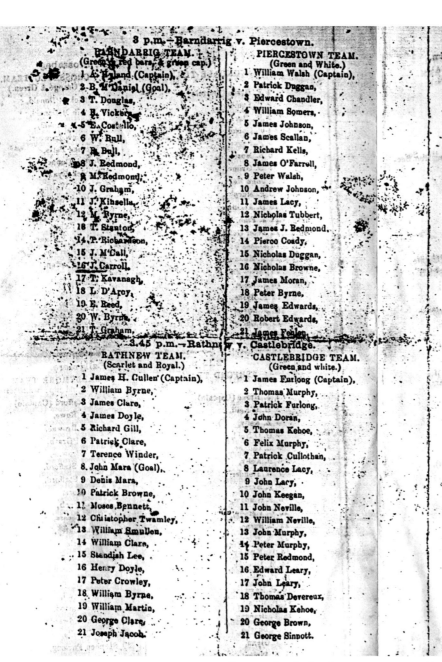

3 p.m.—Barndarrig v. Piercestown.

BARNDARRIG TEAM. (Green & red bars, & green cap.)	PIERCESTOWN TEAM. (Green and White.)
1 A. Byland (Captain),	1 William Walsh (Captain),
2 B. M'Daniel (Goal),	2 Patrick Duggan,
3 T. Douglas,	3 Edward Chandler,
4 R. Vickers,	4 William Somers,
5 E. Costello,	5 James Johnson,
6 W. Bull,	6 James Scallan,
7 R. Bull,	7 Richard Kells,
8 J. Redmond,	8 James O'Farrell,
9 M. Redmond,	9 Peter Walsh,
10 J. Graham,	10 Andrew Johnson,
11 J. Kinsella,	11 James Lacy,
12 L. Byrne,	12 Nicholas Tubbert,
13 T. Stanton,	13 James J. Redmond,
14 P. Richardson,	14 Pierce Coady,
15 J. M'Dall,	15 Nicholas Duggan,
16 J. Carroll,	16 Nicholas Browne,
17 T. Kavanagh,	17 James Moran,
18 L. D'Arcy,	18 Peter Byrne,
19 E. Reed,	19 James Edwards,
20 W. Byrne,	20 Robert Edwards,
21 T. Graham,	21 James Fenlon,

3.45 p.m.—Rathnew v. Castlebridge.

RATHNEW TEAM. (Scarlet and Royal.)	CASTLEBRIDGE TEAM. (Green and white.)
1 James H. Cullen (Captain),	1 James Furlong (Captain),
2 William Byrne,	2 Thomas Murphy,
3 James Clare,	3 Patrick Furlong,
4 James Doyle,	4 John Doran,
5 Richard Gill,	5 Thomas Kehoe,
6 Patrick Clare,	6 Felix Murphy,
7 Terence Winder,	7 Patrick Cullothan,
8 John Mara (Goal),	8 Laurence Lacy,
9 Denis Mara,	9 John Lacy,
10 Patrick Browne,	10 John Keegan,
11 Moses Bennett,	11 John Neville,
12 Christopher Twamley,	12 William Neville,
13 William Smullen,	13 John Murphy,
14 William Clare,	14 Peter Murphy,
15 Standish Lee,	15 Peter Redmond,
16 Henry Doyle,	16 Edward Leary,
17 Peter Crowley,	17 John Leary,
18 William Byrne,	18 Thomas Devereux,
19 William Martin,	19 Nicholas Kehoe,
20 George Clare,	20 George Brown,
21 Joseph Jacob.	21 George Sinnott.

GAELIC ATHLETIC ASSOCIATION.

PROGRAMME

OF THE

FIRST GRAND
INTER-COUNTY CONTEST,
WICKLOW V. WEXFORD,

Under the Rules of the G.A.A.,

AT AVONDALE,

The Seat of the distinguished Leader of the Irish People,

C. S. PARNELL, Esq., M.P.,

ON SUNDAY, 31st OF OCTOBER, 1886,

To commence at 12 o'clock sharp.

GENERAL MANAGERS :
Messrs. E. WALSH, Wexford; and P. M'DONNELL, Bray.

REFEREES :
Messrs. E. J. KENNEDY, V.P., G.A.A., and JOHN CLANCY, T.C., Sub-Sheriff, Dublin.

UMPIRES :
WICKLOW—Mr. PETER ROBINSON, Bray, (Field) ; Messrs. A. M'DANIEL and COLCLOUGH BYRNE (Goals).
WEXFORD—Messrs. P. COUSINS and W. PETTIT (Field) ; N. KAVANAGH, and J. STAFFORD, Wexford ; W. KELLY, Rosslare ; JOHN SCALLAN, Piercestown ; JAMES MURPHY, Crossabeg ; EDMUND PIERCE, Lady's Island (Goal)

TIMEKEEPERS :
WICKLOW—Dr. M. C. DWYER, Rathdrum ; and Mr. LEE CULLEN, Cronakerry.
WEXFORD—Messrs. J. F. WALSH, Wexford ; and M. DOYLE, Cottage.

HON. SECS.—Messrs. P. M'DONNELL and N. KEHOE.

MATCHES AND TEAMS:
The Programme of the Six Matches, commencing at 12 o'clock sharp.
(Time for each Match 40 minutes).

12 o'clock—Wicklow Town v. Wexford Town.
12.45 p.m.—Toghor v. Rosslare.
1.30 p.m.—Avondale v. Crossabeg.
2.15 p.m.—Ashford v. Ballymore.
3 p.m.—Barndarrig v. Piercestown.
3.45 p.m.—Rathnew v. Castlebridge.

Trains—From Wexford, 9.15 a.m. ; from Dublin, 5 p.m. ; from Rathdrum (for Wexford), 6.20 p.m. ; from Rathdrum (for Dublin), 6.20 p.m.

PUBLISHED BY JAMES DWYER, John-st., WEXFORD.

Printed at "The People" Office, Wexford.

Program for the first inter-county competition under GAA rules, held at the estate of Charles Stewart Parnell, October 31, 1886.

GAA teams,
late 1800s.

socialist but also an ardent separatist and admirer of the physical force tradition of Irish republicanism. She had been highly active in the centenary commemoration of the Rebellion of 1798 and was involved in anti-eviction agitation beginning in the 1880s. She was prominent in the formation of the national theater and acted on the Abbey stage. W. B. Yeats was famously in love with her, but she refused him, marrying instead the Boer war hero

When I Was a Little Girl

When I was a little girl
In the garden playing
A thing was often said
To chide us delaying.

When after sunny hours,
at twilight's falling,
down through the garden walks
came our old nurse calling

"Come in! for it's growing late,
And the grass will wet ye!
Come in! or when it's dark
The Fenians will get ye."

Then at this dreadful news,
All helter-skelter
The panic-struck little flock
Ran home for shelter.

And round the nursery fire
Sat still to listen
Fifty bare toes on the hearth
Ten eyes a'glisten

To hear of a night in March
And loyal folk waiting
To see a great army of men
Come devastating.

An army of papists grim
With a green flag o'er them
Redcoats and black police
Flying before them

But God (who our nurse declared
Guards British dominions)
Sent down a fall of snow
And scattered the Fenians.

"But somewhere they're lurking yet
Maybe they're near us,"
Four little hearts pit-a pat
Thought, 'Can they hear us?'

Then the wind-shaken pane
Sounded like drumming;
"Oh!," they cried, "tuck us in
The Fenians are coming."

Four little pairs of hands
In the cots where she led them
Over their frightened heads
Pulled up the bedclothes.

But one little rebel there
Watching all with laughter
Thought 'when the Fenians come
I'll rise and go after.'

Wished she had been a boy
And a good deal older—
Able to walk for miles
With a gun on her shoulder

Able to lift aloft
The green flag o'er them
(red coats and black police
Flying before them).

And as she dropped asleep,
Was wondering whether
God, if they prayed to him
Would give fine weather.

—Alice Milligan[4]

Arthur Griffith addressing a crowd in Dublin.

James Connolly.

Thomas MacDonagh.

Helena Moloney.

Countess Markievicz.

Alice Milligan.

John McBride, whom she soon divorced. (McBride would later be executed for his part in the 1916 Rising). A significant number of the women active in radical nationalist circles, including Countess Markievicz, formerly Constance Gore-Booth, her sister Eva Gore-Booth, and Alice Milligan, shared the same Protestant, largely upper-class unionist backgound.

One of the most important weapons in the arsenal of these radical groups was the fringe press, including *The United Irishman*, edited by Arthur Griffith and to which Maud Gonne was a regular contributor; *Worker's Republic*, edited by James Connolly; the Gaelic League's bilingual paper, *An Claidheamh Solais* (*The Sword of the Light*), edited by Pearse; and in Belfast the *Shan Van Vocht*, which was edited by the poet Alice Milligan. The radical women's organization Inghinidhe na hÉireann (The Daughters of Ireland), founded by Maud Gonne, had its own newspaper, *Bean na hÉireann*, edited by Helena Moloney. Moloney, who would be a leading activist in 1916, was a working-class Dubliner and was responsible for first bringing Constance Gore-Booth, Countess Markievicz, into a militant organization. She was also involved in the Abbey Theatre as an actor and was very close to James Connolly and the socialists.

One of the leading figures in the Gaelic League was Pádraig Pearse. Born in Dublin to an English father, a sculptor, and an Irish mother, the young Pearse excelled in school and won a scholarship to the Royal University, where he took a

above: Members of the Irish Socialist Republican Party with James Connolly (front center with moustache), 1901.

Membership card for the London Branch of Conradh na Gaeilge, 1901.

The Shan Van Vocht.

Yes Ireland shall be free
From the centre to the sea,
And hurrah for Liberty
Says the Shan Van Vocht.

VOL. I.—No. 1. BELFAST, 15TH JANUARY, 1896. PRICE TWOPENCE.

The Shan Van Vocht.

THERE is news from o'er the sea,
    Says the Shan Van Vocht;
There is news from o'er the sea,
    Says the Shan Van Vocht;
And this message o'er the sea,
From the land of liberty,
Brings the best of news for me,
    Says the Shan Van Vocht.

Ere the dying of the year,
    Says the Shan Van Vocht;
From a land that's far but dear
    To the Shan Van Vocht;
In a voice that laughed at fear,
There rang forth defiance clear,
Let us send an answering cheer,
    Says the Shan Van Vocht.

And a cloud is glooming now,
    Says the Shan Van Vocht,
O'er our haughty tyrant's brow,
    Says the Shan Van Vocht;
Whilst like thunder bursts afar,
Where her sons and daughters are,
The din of dreadful war,
    Says the Shan Van Vocht.

But there's light behind that cloud
    For the Shan Van Vocht;
And that thunder roaring loud,
    Says the Shan Van Vocht;
Though it strikes the weakling dumb,
Shouts in tones of joy to some
That the dawn of Freedom's come
    To the Shan Van Vocht.

But tell me who is she
    Called the Shan Van Vocht;
And if other name there be
    For the Shan Van Vocht;
Yes! immortal is her fame,
She's the queen no foe could tame,
For old Ireland is the name
    Of the Shan Van Vocht.

The Boy From Barnesmore.

(A STORY OF '67.) BY IRIS OLKYRN.

THE train had stopped an unusually long time at Strabane Station. Trains in Ireland are rarely in a hurry; indeed, when you come to think of it why should they be, as some wit remarked "there is more time to spare than there is of anything else in this distressful country." And to-day there was every excuse for delay, and plenty to divert my attention whilst we waited, for that day had been the great spring hiring market in Strabane, and the crowd upon the platform was an interesting and picturesque one.

Here were the wives of strong farmers in all the flaunting bravery of their new spring bonnets, gorgeous in scarlet and purple, and emerald green ribbons with wondrous flowers, fresh from the milliners' hands; whilst in paper bags they carried the head-dresses in which they had come to town that morning. Their crinoline distended skirts, their gay fringed shawls, their loudly creaking boots, were objects of wonder and envy to the simply dressed country girls of Donegal, who had entered into six months service with them that day, and who had left homes among the mountain glens up by Stranorlar and Glenties, and far away in Gweedore, to do housework and field work on farms in Tyrone. I could not help admiring the picturesque simplicity of their plain kilted skirts of grey or dark blue homespun; the bright kerchiefs knotted simply over their neatly braided locks as compared with the tawdry grandeur of their newly found mistresses. The men were shouting and talking excitedly, running this way and that, and calling to their women folk to follow to the seats they had secured in the carriages. Through the swaying, surging crowd, with quiet sauntering step passed two or three straight military looking men, easily recognised as members of the police force in plain clothes. I thought nothing of their passing up and down and

---

Bean na h=Eireann.

THE WOMAN OF IRELAND.

THE PAPER FOR ALL IRISHWOMEN.

Published Monthly. | **Price One Penny.**

bean na h-éireann is a Paper for all Irishwomen who recognise that they have a duty to their country.

ORDER FORM.

To the Manager, bean na h-éireann,

22 North Great George's Street,

DUBLIN.

Please send me _____ *copies of* bean na h-éireann *for* _____

months, dating from _____

      Name _____

      Address _____

Subscription rates—1s. 6d. for one year, post free. American Subscribers 50 cents. a year, payable in advance.

FLEASE SEND POSTAL ORDER OR **HALF-PENNY** STAMPS.

left: The first edition of the *Shan Van Vocht*, published in Belfast, January 15, 1896.

right: Order form for *Bean na hÉireann.*

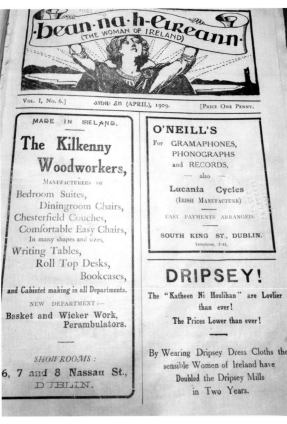

degree in Arts and Law and was later called to the Irish Bar. He joined the Gaelic League shortly after leaving school and soon became prominent in cultural nationalist circles. He became editor of *An Claidheamh Solais*, the newspaper of the League. He was also a prolific writer in both Irish and English, although he strongly believed that a truly national literature would of necessity be in the Irish language and was a passionate proponent of the importance of the language to any sense of national identity. One of the main forces he identi-

fied as contributing to anglicization and weakening the national and indeed human spirit was the educational system, attacked in his pamphlet "The Murder Machine." Pearse was not only an idealist, however, he was also a man of action. In 1908, on a shoestring budget, he founded St Enda's, a bilingual school for boys, where he put his principles into practice. Celtic myth and legend formed an important part of the curriculum of the school. St Enda's was to become a hotbed of revolutionary nationalism. Fifteen former pupils along with four

left: Front page of *Bean na hÉireann,* April 1909.

center: Page from *Bean na hÉireann* showing an advertisement for Pearse's school, St Enda's.

right: Nationalist Women's Association flyer.

above: Façade of the old Abbey Theatre, 1913.

above right: Playbill for the Irish National Theatre Society at the Abbey Theatre, 1905.

right: Kathleen Ni Houlihan, Abbey stage, 1902, with Maud Gonne (far right) in leading role.

teachers were to take part in the 1916 rebellion. All four teachers, Pearse himself, his younger brother Willie, Thomas MacDonagh, and Con Colbert would be executed for their parts in the rebellion.

Thomas MacDonagh was one of Pearse's first teaching colleagues in St Enda's. A native of Cloughjordan, County Tipperary, he was also appointed to a lectureship at University College Dublin in English literature. MacDonagh had also been active in the Gaelic League. He was prominent in literary circles and wrote prolifically in many different genres: prose, poetry, and drama. He was close to the poet William Butler Yeats,

below: Con Colbert conducting drill with boys in St Enda's.

right: Willie and Pádraig Pearse.

Éamonn Ceannt, adjudicator (front center, slightly to the right, with moustache), with pipers at the Oireachtas, Rotunda, Dublin, ca. 1900.

whom he looked upon as his mentor. Other figures in these circles included Joseph Mary Plunkett, the son of a papal count, who cut a flamboyant figure and was taught Irish by Thomas Mac-Donagh. They were both involved in setting up the Irish Theatre Company and a journal, *The Irish Review*.

While Pearse and his fellow Gaelic Leaguers had initially dedicated themselves to cultural activism, they were increasingly drawn in the direction of political action. During George V's 1911

visit, Pearse, along with MacDonagh and another prominent member of cultural nationalist circles, Éamonn Ceannt, who was a noted piper and language activist, were involved in a campaign to stop Dublin Corporation from presenting a loyal address to Parliament. This was, in the words of one of his contemporaries, the first time he had taken "an open part in politics as distinct from the language and cultural movements." It would not be the last. More and more, the new generation of cultural nationalists were being inspired by the ideas

left: Robert Emmet.

right: Patriots of 1798.

of separatism and republicanism, drawing inspiration from a tradition of resistance to British rule that they traced from Wolfe Tone and the United Irishmen to Robert Emmet and Young Ireland to the Fenians.

Fenianism had been an inexorable part of Irish political life since the mid-nineteenth century. Taking over where previous separatist movements such as the United Irishmen and Young Ireland left off, it had been formally constituted as the

IRB, the Irish Republican Brotherhood, but was more commonly referred to as the "Fenians," based on the name of the hero of medieval Irish literature Fionn Mac Cumhail and his mythical band of warriors, Na Fianna. The Fenians were pledged to an independent Irish republic established by force of arms.

Fenianism had also been inspired by revolutionary ideas from Europe, following the example of previous Irish separatists. The Catholic

O Church and King in close embrace
The burden of the human race
the people tell you to their face
that soon you will repent it
For King and power and teaching drones
The source of all our heavy groans
Down from your pulpits and your
thrones
You will tumble unlamented.
—The Carmagnols
(French revolutionary ballad)[5]

left: Depiction of French Revolution by Eugene Delacroix, *La liberté guidant le peuple.*

right: Wolfe Tone pleads Ireland's case with Napoleon.

hierarchy with one or two exceptions had been vehemently opposed to the Fenians in the late nineteenth century. Bishop Moriarty of Kerry, for example, famously denounced the Fenian leadership in a pastoral letter, stating that "hell was not hot enough nor eternity long enough to punish these miscreants."

Irish revolutionaries were not insular in outlook. As they did for the 1867 Fenian Rising, they had long looked beyond their own shores for aid, which on those few occasions when given was too little and too late, but especially for inspiration. The United Irishmen had been inspired by the egalitarian and republican ideals of the French Revolution. France continued to provide a refuge and an inspiration to all manner of European radicals, including antimonarchists and republicans from Poland, Italy, and not least Ireland throughout the nineteenth century. Paris was often said to be the capital of Irish republicanism up to the 1880s.

Although some of the new revolutionary generation, including Maud Gonne, Countess Markievicz, and Helena Moloney, also spent time in France, the focus and energy were to shift to the Irish diaspora, "that Irish nation of discontent beyond the seas," as Prime Minister Gladstone put it. While many Irish emigrants populated British cities such as London, Manchester, Liverpool, and Glasgow, by far the most important center of political activity was among the vast numbers of the Irish diaspora in the United States.

The Fenian Proclamation, 1867

We have suffered centuries of outrage, enforced poverty, and bitter misery. Our rights and liberties have been trampled on by an alien aristocracy, who treating us as foes, usurped our lands, and drew away from our unfortunate country all material riches. The real owners of the soil were removed to make room for cattle, and driven across the ocean to seek the means of living, and the political rights denied to them at home, while our men of thought and action were condemned to loss of life and liberty. But we never lost the memory and hope of a national existence. We appealed in vain to the reason and sense of justice of the dominant powers. Our mildest remonstrances were met with sneers and contempt. Our appeals to arms were always unsuccessful.

Today, having no honourable alternative left, we again appeal to force as our last resource. We accept the conditions of appeal, manfully deeming it better to die in the struggle for freedom than to continue an existence of utter serfdom.

All men are born with equal rights, and in associating to protect one another and share public burdens, justice demands that such associations should rest upon a basis which maintains equality instead of destroying it.

We therefore declare that, unable longer to endure the curse of Monarchical Government, we aim at founding a Republic based on universal suffrage, which shall secure to all the intrinsic value of their labour.

The soil of Ireland, at present in the possession of an oligarchy, belongs to us, the Irish people, and to us it must be restored.

We declare, also, in favour of absolute liberty of conscience, and complete separation of Church and State.

We appeal to the Highest Tribunal for evidence of the justness of our cause. History bears testimony to the integrity of our sufferings, and we declare, in the face of our brethren, that we intend no war against the people of England—our war is against the aristocratic locusts, whether English or Irish, who have eaten the verdure of our fields—against the aristocratic leeches who drain alike our fields and theirs.

Republicans of the entire world, our cause is your cause. Our enemy is your enemy. Let your hearts be with us. As for you, workmen of England, it is not only your hearts we wish, but your arms. Remember the starvation and degradation brought to your firesides by the oppression of labour. Remember the past, look well to the future, and avenge yourselves by giving liberty to your children in the coming struggle for human liberty.

Herewith we proclaim the Irish Republic.

We've men from the Nore, from the Suir and the Shannon,
Let tyrants come forth, we'll bring force against force.
Our pen is our sword and our voice is our cannon
Rifle for rifle and horse against horse.
We've made the false Saxon yield
Many a red battlefield:
God on our side we will triumph again;
Pay them back woe for woe
Give them back blow for blow—
Out and make way for the Bold Fenian Men
                    —from "The Bold Fenian Men"
                           (popular ballad)[6]

The Fenian Banner, 1866.

The American Connection

Although there had long been a tradition of Irish emigration to America, in particular among the Protestant population, or Scots-Irish as they were known, it was the mass emigration of Catholic Irish after the Great Famine that would leave an indelible mark. By the early 1900s, the Irish, remarkably, constituted 20 percent of the overall population of the United States. In major cities such as New York, Chicago, Boston, and Philadelphia, however, the percentage was considerably higher. Since the 1860s a number of Irish American organizations had been active in supporting the nationalist cause in Ireland. Some supported the constitutional Home Rule movement, while others followed the separatist gospel of the Fenians.

This latter group, marked with a deep antipathy to Britain, provided impetus for the regeneration of the physical force republican tradition within Ireland. Clan na Gael (known in Ireland as the Irish Republican Brotherhood) would supply both moral and financial support for the overthrow

Irish immigrants in the U.S., 1909.

O father dear I oftimes hear you speak of
   Erin's isle
Her lofty scenes, her valleys green, her
   mountains rude and wild
They say it is a lovely land wherein a prince
   might dwell
So why did you abandon it the reason to me
   tell?

My son I loved my native land with energy
   and pride
Till a blight came over all my crops and my
   sheep and cattle died
The rent and taxes were to pay and I could
   not them redeem
And that's the cruel reason why I left old
   Skibbereen.

Then sadly I recall the days of gloomy forty
   eight
I rose in vengeance with the boys to battle
   against fate
We were hunted through the mountains as
   traitors to the Queen
And that my boy is the reason why I left old
   Skibbereen.

Well father dear the day will come when on
   vengeance we will call
And Irishmen both stout and tall will rally
   unto the call
I'll be the man to lead the van beneath the
   flag of green
And loud and high we'll raise the cry
   'Revenge for Skibbereen'.

—"Skibbereen"
(popular ballad)[7]

of British rule and the establishment of an Irish republic. Many of the leading figures had come to the United States as political exiles and had been active in separatist politics in Ireland. Foremost among them was the figure of John Devoy, a dedicated advocate of Irish separatism in America. Once described as Ireland's Lenin, he had been active in Irish revolutionary circles in Paris as a young man. He became an active Fenian, was imprisoned, and then released under condition of exile and subsequently arrived in the U.S.

John Devoy soon became prominent in Clan na Gael and was the editor of two influential newspapers, the *Irish Nation* and later the *Gaelic American*, which spread the doctrine of Irish freedom among a sympathetic audience. Many of these Irish Americans had taken part in the American Civil War. They fought on both sides, although the majority fought for the Union. After the Civil War many who had fought were prepared to devote their military experience to the cause of their native land. By 1867 plans had been laid. A ship, *Erin's Hope*, was readied to bring arms and men as reinforcements to Ireland for a planned insurrection. The Fenian Rising of 1867 was a military fiasco. The day on which it was to happen had the heaviest snowfall in Ireland in fifty years. The papers recorded that "A perfect tempest of hail and snow swept the land." The rising was also a debacle, doomed to failure because the conspirators had been thoroughly infiltrated by informers.

Despite the total failure in Ireland, the Fenians in America did not lose heart. They attempted

Immigrants arrive at Ellis Island, New York, 1902.

a number of raids into Canada. They hoped to get the British to agree to give Ireland independence or else provoke an American-British war. Unnerved by the activity on her borders, the U.S. government stepped in and the raids ceased. But the American Fenians continued to organize and support resistance to British rule in Ireland. In the 1880s they decided to strike at the heart of the British empire. The streets of British cities were to become their battleground. Organized and planned by Jeremiah O'Donovan Rossa, the aim of the Dynamite War, as it became known, was to terrorize Britain and to focus public attention on Ireland. Young men were dispatched from Ireland and the United States to bomb British cities. Again,

Ireland's opportunity will come when England is engaged in a desperate struggle with some great European power or European combination or when the flame of insurrection has spread through her Indian empire, and her strength and resources are strained.

—John Devoy,
commenting on the optimum
timing of a rebellion[8]

top: John Devoy.

Chaplain and men of the Irish Brigade during the American Civil War.

From Erin's soil the Saxon foe
In shame shall be forever driven;
From Erin's sons who bear the woe,
The tyrants chain shall soon be riven;
And Erin's emerald isle shall be,
The Gem of Freedom in the sea.

FREEDOM TO IRELAND.

Then up and arm at Erin's call,
Ye FENIAN sons of Irish sires;
On every hill and mountain tall,
Arise and light your signal fires.
And swear to win with heart and hand.
The Freedom of your Native land.

NEW YORK, PUBD BY CURRIER & IVES. 152 NASSAU ST

left: Fenian poster.

above: Depiction of the Fenian ship
Erin's Hope.

British intelligence was up to the job. Many of the bombers and conspirators were quickly arrested. Among them was a young man named Tom Clarke. Clarke would become the father figure of the 1916 Rising, the link between Fenianism and the new generation.

In many ways, Tom Clarke personified the physical force tradition of Irish republicanism. He was born in the Isle of Wight, where his father was in the British Army, and later moved back to County Tyrone, to Dungannon, where he grew up. He joined the IRB and then went to America in late 1880, where he met John Devoy and joined Clan na Gael, as the IRB was known in the U.S. Two years later he was sent to England to take part in the bombing campaign. He was arrested and sentenced to life imprisonment. Having served fifteen and a half years under harsh conditions, Clarke was released as part of a general amnesty for Fenian prisoners. Bent, stooped, and prematurely aged, he nonetheless remained a proud and unrepentant Fenian.

Upon his release in 1898, Tom Clarke immediately returned to America. Reconnecting with John Devoy, he resumed his activities with Clan na Gael with an even more heightened sense of commitment. In 1901 Clarke married a young woman from Limerick, Kathleen Daly, whose uncle John Daly had been in prison with him and who shared his republican principles. In 1905 Clarke became an American citizen, working closely with Devoy on the *Gaelic American*. Like their predecessors in the United Irishmen who looked to republican France for military aid, Clan na Gael looked to the international situation to assist them in their anti-British efforts. Speculation was rife in the American press of an impending European war, and Devoy, Clarke, and their comrades in Clan na Gael were determined to be ready in such an event. Ireland needed to be prepared. Despite Kathleen Clarke's initial misgivings, Tom Clarke returned to Dublin with his family in 1907 with Devoy's blessing. His task was to revitalize the IRB. The

left: Tom Clarke in 1883.

above: Jeremiah O'Donovan Rossa.

Clarkes purchased a small tobacconist shop in Dublin's Parnell Street, which would become the de facto headquarters of the clandestine republican movement. It became a center of sedition. Soon after his return, Clarke met a young man named Seán Mac Diarmada from County Leitrim, who had joined the IRB while working as a tram driver in Belfast. Mac Diarmada moved to, and he and Clarke became close friends. With Clarke's steely commitment and Mac Diarmada's unfailing energy, they would reinvigorate the physical force tradition. Mac Diarmada would be at Clarke's side to the end.

Back in America, Devoy and Clan na Gael kept up their work. Devoy opened the pages of the *Gaelic American* to other anticolonial activists, Indian and Egyptian nationalists in particular. America had long acted as a republican exemplar and template for emerging anti-imperialist movements, and cities such as New York and San Francisco were meeting points for clandestine activists to show solidarity with one another.

Back in Ireland, many of those who identified with the separatist and radical tendencies also continued to draw clear analogies between their struggle and that of other colonial peoples. The story of rebellion and of the often brutal suppression in India and other colonies had clear parallels for them in Irish history. Their common enemy was the British Empire.

I could see that this talk of England being engaged in war in the near future was having an unsettling effect on Tom. Night after night, sitting down when work was done, he would revert to it, and the tragedy it would be if Ireland failed to avail herself of such an opportunity to make a bid for freedom. If she failed to do so, it would break the tradition of generations, and might end in Ireland becoming resigned to her fate as part of the British Empire. The thought of such a thing happening was to him intolerable; to avert that fate from the country he loved he was ready to sacrifice everything, self, wife, child.

—Kathleen Clarke, from her autobiography[9]

top: Kathleen Clarke.

Seán Mac Diarmada.

The Daughters of Ireland and Mother India

On July 1, 1909, at a function in London hosted by the Indian National Association, a young Indian revolutionary nationalist assassinated Sir Curzon Wyllie, the political aide-de-camp to the secretary of state for India. Madan Lal Dhingra, a student at University College London, was a scion of a wealthy loyalist family from the Punjab. He was arrested, tried for murder, and sentenced to death. He was hanged in Pentonville Prison by the official executioner, H. A. Pierrepoint, on August 17. In his statement to the court, Dhingra justified his actions in tones reminiscent of numerous Irish rebels from Wolfe Tone to Robert Emmet to the most recent patriot dead, William Philip Allen, Michael Larkin, and Michael O'Brien, known to Irish nationalists as the Manchester Martyrs. They were Fenian prisoners who had been publicly executed outside Salford Prison in Manchester some forty years earlier.

Madan Lal Dhingra's death did not go unmarked by Irish anti-imperialists. In Dublin, members of Inghindhe na hÉireann, including Maud Gonne and Helena Moloney, quickly printed and posted flyers acknowledging Dhingra as an Indian patriot and martyr. Questions were asked in outraged tones at Westminster about Irish republican propaganda honoring the executed Indian.

Madan Lal Dhingra.

opposite: A poster commemorating the Manchester Martyrs, William Allen, Michael Larkin, and Michael O'Brien, executed November 23, 1867.

I will die proudly and triumphantly in defence of republican principle and the liberty of an oppressed and enslaved people. God Save Ireland—

—Speech from the dock by William Allen, one of the three Manchester Martyrs publicly hung outside Salford Prison, Manchester, 1867

High upon the gallows tree swung the noble-hearted three,
By the vengeful tyrant stricken in their bloom
But they met him face to face with the courage of their race
And they went with souls undaunted to their doom.

'God save Ireland' said the heroes,
'God save Ireland' said they all
Whether on the scaffold high
Or the battlefield we die
Oh what matter when for Ireland dear we fall.

—"God Save Ireland" (popular ballad)[10]

I believe that a nation held down by foreign bayonets is in a perpetual state of war. Since open battle is rendered impossible to a disarmed race, I attacked by surprise. Since guns were denied to me I drew forth my pistol and fired. Poor in health and intellect, a son like myself has nothing else to offer to the mother but his own blood. And so I have sacrificed the same on her altar. The only lesson required in India at present is to learn how to die, and the only way to teach it is by dying ourselves. My only prayer to God is that I may be reborn of the same mother and I may re-die in the same sacred cause till the cause is successful.

I am proud to have the honour of laying down my life for my country. But remember we shall have our time in the days to come.

—Madan Lal Dhingra's speech from the dock, 1909

While those years preceding the first World War are now regarded as quiet years, the Inghinidhe kept up its work of teaching, anti-enlisting, and anti-British propaganda. For instance, about this time a young Indian revolutionary, Madar [Madan] Lal Dhingra, was captured and hanged for complicity in the assassination of a prominent Indian Police official. From the dock, when sentenced, he declared, "I am proud to lay down my life for my country." We got printed immediately, and fly-posted through the city, posters stating "Ireland honours Madar Lal Dhingra, who was proud to lay down his life for his country". There was nothing insular about Inghinidhe's political outlook. We reproduced this poster in "Bean na hÉireann", and it resulted in the loss of some advertisements and subscriptions.

—Helena Moloney,
witness statement[11]

SPEAKER OF THE HOUSE
The right honorable Captain Craig
CRAIG
I wish to ask the honourable member, the Chief Secretary for Ireland, whether his attention has been drawn to the fact that placards have been extensively posted throughout certain parts of Ireland to the effect that "Ireland honours Madar Lal Dhingra, who was proud to lay down his life for the cause of his country"; and whether the police have discovered the authors of the placards praising a murderer; and if so have any arrests been made?

SPEAKER OF THE HOUSE
The Right Honorable Mr Cherry
CHERRY
I am informed by the police authorities that a number of such placards were found posted in various parts of Ireland and were at once torn down by the police. The authors have not so far been discovered, nor have any arrests been made

—Hansard account of exchange
in House of Commons,
Westminster

IRELAND
———
A Scandalous Placard.
Dublin, Aug. 18.
Last night a large placard was posted within a mile of the city of Dublin on the main road leading from the city to Malahide, which bore the following inscription in big type:—
"Ireland honours Madar Lal Dhingra, who was proud to lay down his life for the cause of his country."
The poster bore no imprint and there was no clue as to its origin. It appears that a similar placard has been posted up in other parts of the country.

—*Times*, London,
August 18, 1909

"We'll Keep the Red Flag Flying"

HELENA MOLONEY'S RADICAL VIEWS WERE shared to a greater or lesser extent by Tom Clarke and his IRB comrades but also by the increasingly militant and anti-imperialist stance of the labor movement under James Connolly. Like Clarke, James Connolly was a very interesting figure. Again like Clarke, he was a product of the diaspora, and both his parents were Irish. He was brought up in the slums of Glasgow, in a part called "Little Ireland." Connolly joined the British Army at the age of fourteen and was sent to Ireland but became politicized very quickly. He developed an intense hatred of landlordism. He was self-educated and combined from the beginning socialist principles with a strong sense of Irish republicanism. In Dublin he founded a new party, which he called the Irish Socialist Republican Party. Connolly made common cause with other radicals and was at the forefront of protests against Victoria's visit and the Boer War and was arrested on both occasions. Close to activists like Maud Gonne, Helena Moloney, and Alice Milligan, Connolly was a strong supporter of suffrage and committed to women's rights.

In 1903 Connolly had moved to the United States, where he was joined by his wife, Lily, and their young family. They settled in Newark, New

The struggle for Irish freedom has two aspects: it is national and it is social. The national idea can never be realized until Ireland stands forth before the world as a nation, free and independent. It is social and economic, because no matter what form the government may be, as long as one class owns as private property the land and instruments of labour from which mankind derive their substance, that class will always have it in their power to plunder and enslave the kinder of their fellow creatures.

—James Connolly,
in *The Harp*, 1908

Handbill advertising "the Irish American Orator" James Connolly, 1910.

Jersey. Connolly joined the Industrial Workers of the World, the Wobblies, as they were known, touring large areas of the U.S. as a union organizer. He remained committed to Irish radical republicanism, founding the Irish Socialist Foundation and editing its newspaper, *The Harp*.

By the end of 1910 Connolly was back in Ireland. He was living in Belfast and working as an organizer for the Irish Transport and General Workers Union, the first trade union for general and unskilled workers in Ireland. He would later move to Dublin, his commitment to an imminent socialist and national revolution deepening by the day.

James Connolly addressing a May Day rally in New York City, 1908.

The "Irish Question"

DESPITE THE EFFORTS OF RADICAL SEPARATISTS, the Fenian tradition of armed opposition to Britain was very much a minority pastime in the first decade of the twentieth century. The vast majority of Irish people identified as nationalist, which was, for the most part, synonymous with Catholic. The majority of nationalists supported the Irish Party, which had been united under the leadership of John Redmond following the splits and feuds after the demise of Parnell. Their demand was for Home Rule. Redmond and the Irish Party sought to achieve this by playing the parliamentary game in Westminster, supporting the Liberal Party. The Liberals had traditionally been supportive of reforms in Ireland both in terms of land reforms, which had been one of the major causes of dissent in Ireland in the previous century, and also constitutional reform, which was opposed strongly by the Conservative Party and by the Irish Unionist MPs.

By 1911 the rumblings of the political and cultural forces at play in what the British referred to as the "Irish Question" were beginning to be clearly heard. Since the 1870s the demand for Home Rule in Ireland, which entailed a limited form of self-government, had been a central tenet of the Irish Parliamentary Party and constitutional nationalism generally. Ireland had been without a parliament of its own since the Dublin Parliament

John Redmond, the hero of Home Rule.

was abolished by the Act of Union in 1800 following the rebellion of 1798. From then on, political control of Ireland resided in London and was administered from Dublin Castle.

Moreover, the acrimonious splits of the Parnell era, which had fractured nationalist Ireland, were beginning to be healed, and the Home Rule movement was gaining increasing momentum under the leadership of John Redmond. Redmond did not have the charisma of Parnell, but he had managed to unite the Irish Party and turn it into a cohesive and successful vehicle in Westminster. And although he had opposed the Boer War, he remained a strong supporter of Ireland's role within the British Empire. For Redmond, as for many constitutional nationalists, Home Rule would not entail separation from Britain and leaving the empire, but would mean self-government within the empire, like the dominion status of Australia and Canada, the "white colonies" who were trusted to rule themselves within the imperial framework. For others who supported Home Rule, it was a step on the way to greater independence.

Irish nationalism and the Home Rule movement of the time were neither homogenous nor ideologically unified. They attracted the support of people whose views ranged from being pro-empire, conservative, and pro-clerical, such as those of John Redmond himself, to those nationalists who in the past had held Fenian sympathies or had been active in the land war.

The vast majority of Home Rule sympathizers did not necessarily see Home Rule as their ultimate goal. This inherent ambiguity allowed the Home Rule movement to draw on a broad base, from the burgeoning Catholic middle classes anxious to do well for themselves within the imperial project to those of a more separatist persuasion but who saw a Home Rule parliament in Dublin as the means to an end.

Indeed, three months after thousands thronged the streets of Dublin to see the royal procession, another large crowd gathered in the center of Dublin, this time to see John Redmond unveil a statue of Charles Stewart Parnell, the (Protestant) former leader of nationalist Ireland. The base of the statue held an inscription, a quotation from Parnell: "No man has a right to fix the boundary to the march of a nation. No man has a right to say to his country thus far shalt thou go and no further." It was a clear enunciation of the ongoing sentiments of much of nationalist Ireland.

Charles Stewart Parnell.

The Unionist Response

BY 1912 IT SEEMED THAT THE PASSING OF Home Rule was simply a matter of time. The Irish Party of John Redmond held the balance of power in Westminster, and the ruling Liberal Party had given a commitment to introducing the third Home Rule Bill in April 1912. Irish unionists, particularly in Ulster, were adamant in their opposition. As the move towards finally passing a Home Rule Bill gathered momentum (previous attempts had been made in 1896 and 1893), unionist reaction was swift and furious. Inspired by the leadership of Sir Edward Carson and James Craig, unionists in Ulster threatened open rebellion if Home Rule were passed.

In many ways Carson was an unlikely leader of Ulster unionism. He was a Dubliner and MP for Trinity College, the bastion of southern unionism. He had made his reputation at the London Bar,

> We must be prepared, in the event of a Home Rule Bill passing, with such measures as will carry on for ourselves the government of those districts of which we have control. We must be prepared—and time is precious in these things—the morning Home Rule passes, ourselves to become responsible for the government of the Protestant Province of Ulster.
> —Edward Carson, addressing a large demonstration outside James Craig's home in East Belfast, September 23, 1911

Sir Edward Carson putting the first signature to the Ulster Covenant, City Hall, Belfast, September 28, 1912. James Craig stands to his left.

opposite: Carson inspecting members of the Ulster Volunteer Force.

famously prosecuting his fellow Irishman Oscar Wilde in one of the most sensationalist trials of the time. He and Craig made a formidable team: Craig had a talent for organization and tactics; Carson had great charisma and was a powerful public speaker. They attracted widespread support among unionists.

Over 400,000 people, including civil servants, soldiers, and police, signed a document known as the Ulster Covenant, pledging themselves to oppose Home Rule, "using all means which may be found necessary to defeat the present conspiracy to set up a Home Rule Parliament in Ireland."

Despite Carson's opposition to suffrage, women also took an active role in organizing against Home Rule. In defiance of convention, some, such as Lady Londonderry, were prominent in the leadership of unionism. Over 100,000 women were active in organizations such as the Ulster Women's Unionist Council, and large numbers signed the Women's Covenant. By now Irish unionism increasingly meant Ulster unionism. Even Edward Carson, himself a southerner, was toying with the idea of partition or secession in the event of Home Rule being passed into law.

By 1913 unionist opposition to Home Rule was becoming increasingly extreme in tone and military in nature. In January, an armed militia, the Ulster Volunteer Force (UVF), was formally mobilized under the slogan, "Ulster will fight and

It has been publicly stated by Sir Edward Carson and others that, in the event of the Bill becoming law, a Provisional Government will forthwith be set up to administer Ulster. The functions of this Government have not been defined, but the Unionist Council will assemble next month to consider the necessary arrangements. The Provisional Government, it is understood, will decide the nature of the resistance to be offered.

The important question now arises, what will be the probable outcome of the movement under discussion. Home rule had now become as much a question of religion as of politics. The sharp and growing antagonism between Protestants and Catholics was clearly shown at Belfast in the summer of last year, and also quite recently at Londonderry. The crisis, as the County Inspector of Antrim remarks, 'has brought together, as never before, the whole Protestant population of the province, and has welded the Protestant churches together by a community of interest and feeling which it would have taken at least a generation under other circumstances to bring about.'
—Inspector General's Monthly Confidential Report, March 1914[12]

Ulster, 1912

The dark eleventh hour
Draws on and sees us sold
To every evil power
We fought against of old.
Rebellion, rapine, hate,
Oppression, wrong, and greed
Are loosed to rule our fate,
By England's act and deed.

The Faith in which we stand,
The laws we made and guard,
Our honour, lives, and land
Are given for reward
To Murder done by night,
To Treason taught by day,
To folly, sloth, and spite,
And we are thrust away.

The blood our fathers spilt,
Our love, our toils, our pains,
Are counted us for guilt,
And only bind our chains.
Before an Empire's eyes
The traitor claims his price.
What need of further lies?
We are the sacrifice.

We asked no more than leave
To reap where we had sown,
Through good and ill to cleave
To our own flag and throne.
Now England's shot and steel
Beneath that flag must show
How loyal hearts should kneel
To England's oldest foe.

We know the war prepared
On every peaceful home,
We know the hells declared
For such as serve not Rome—
The terror, threats, and dread
In market, hearth, and field—
We know, when all is said,
We perish if we yield.

Believe, we dare not boast,
Believe, we do not fear—
We stand to pay the cost
In all that men hold dear.
What answer from the North?
One Law, one Land, one Throne.
If England drive us forth
We shall not fall alone!

—Rudyard Kipling[13]

Solemn League and Covenant (Ulster Covenant)

Being convinced in our consciences that Home Rule would be disastrous to the material well-being of Ulster as well as the whole of Ireland, subversive of our civil and religious freedom, destructive of our citizenship, and perilous to the unity of the Empire, we, whose names are underwritten, men of Ulster, loyal subjects of His Gracious Majesty King George V, humbly relying on the God whom our fathers in days of stress and trial confidently trusted, do hereby pledge ourselves in solemn covenant throughout this our time of threatened calamity to stand by one another in defending for ourselves and our children our cherished position of equal citizenship in the United Kingdom, and in using all means which may be found necessary to defeat the present conspiracy to set up a Home Rule Parliament in Ireland. And in the event such a Parliament being forced upon us we further solemnly and mutually pledge ourselves to refuse to recognise its authority. In sure confidence that God will defend the right we hereto subscribe our names. And further, we individually declare that we have not already signed this covenant. God Save the King.

—written by James Craig

Home Rule means to you that you are to be put under the heel of a majority, which, if greater than you in numbers, is most undoubtedly inferior to you in political knowledge and experience. It means that the whole patronage of Ulster is to be handed over to a hostile majority in Dublin. You, the wealthy, the orderly, the industrious, the enterprising portion of Ireland are to supply the money for that part of Ireland which is less orderly, less industrious, less enterprising and less law-abiding.

—Lord Balfour, speaking to Ulster unionists

Women's Covenant

We, whose names are underwritten, women of Ulster, and loyal subjects of our gracious King, being firmly persuaded that Home Rule would be disastrous to our Country, desire to associate ourselves with the men of Ulster in their uncompromising opposition to the Home Rule Bill now before Parliament, whereby it is proposed to drive Ulster out of her cherished place in the Constitution of the United Kingdom and to place her under the domination and control of a Parliament in Ireland. Praying that from this calamity God will save Ireland, we hereto subscribe our names.

Ulster will be right." "Home Rule means Rome Rule" became another popular mantra. The unionists were supported by the British Conservative Party, who were now in opposition in Westminster. The Conservatives found it politic to "play the orange card," that is, to side with the Ulster unionists. Many well-placed supporters of unionism spoke out against Home Rule. Most prominent were Andrew Bonar Law and Sir Randolph Churchill, both leading members of the Conservative Party. Rudyard Kipling, the unofficial poet laureate of the empire, published a poem in the *Morning Post* enunciating the unionist position.

Despite the overt threats and the ongoing marching and drilling of the Ulster Volunteer Force, the government took no action against them. But the UVF did provoke a reaction within nationalist circles. The opposition of unionism to the proposed Home Rule Bill would lead inexorably to the militarization of nationalist politics.

top left: Carson addressing an anti–Home Rule rally.

top right: Anti–Home Rule postcard representing "Donegall Place, Belfast, under Home Rule."

"Stand Back Redmond" anti–Home Rule postcard.

The Response of Nationalism

IF UNIONISM HAD THE ULSTER VOLUNTEER Force, then nationalist Ireland would have its own militia. On November 25, 1912, thousands of people attended a public meeting at the Rotunda Hospital in Dublin. The outcome of the meeting was the formation of the Irish Volunteers under the leadership of Eoin MacNeill, a founding member of the Gaelic League and the first professor of early and medieval Irish history at University College Dublin, where one of his colleagues was Thomas MacDonagh.

Their manifesto sought to make clear that the Ulster Volunteer Force was not the target of this new force but rather that they were opposing the Conservative Party, which had conspired to "make the display of military force and the menace of armed violence the determining factor in the future relations between Britain and Ireland." Other prominent nationalists, such as Pearse, MacDonagh, Plunkett, and a young mathematics teacher and Gaelic Leaguer named Éamon de Valera, were among the some four thousand men who enrolled on that evening.

Another among the thousands who thronged the Rotunda was Tom Clarke. As befitting the secretive and clandestine nature of the IRB, Clarke was not on the platform but stayed in the wings,

observing. He later wrote approvingly to John Devoy in America of the increasing militancy of Irish nationalists.

From the beginning the IRB had its men in key positions in the Irish Volunteers. One of these was Bulmer Hobson. He was one of the most prominent figures in radical nationalist circles at the time. He had been born in Belfast and educated at a Quaker school. He had cofounded the Dungannon Clubs, a group dedicated to promoting nationalism in the north. In many ways he exemplified the radical activist of the time. He was active in the Gaelic League, the GAA, and the Ulster Literary Theatre and was for a time vice president of Sinn Féin. All of these organizations had been infiltrated by the newly energized IRB after Clarke returned from America. Bulmer Hobson was also to found Na Fianna Éireann, the republican youth movement, along with Countess Markievicz and Helena Moloney. He also became a leading member of the Irish Volunteers.

Among those nationalists attracted to the Irish Volunteers was another Protestant nationalist, Roger Casement. Casement had been born in Dublin, the son of an officer in the British Army. He joined the British consular service as a young man and was posted to Africa. What he saw in the

Joe, it is worth living in Ireland these times—there is an awakening—the slow, silent plodding and the open preaching is at last showing results. . . .

I can't—I won't try to give you a history of the causes that have brought about what I refer to—just take it for granted that the prospect today from the national point of view is brighter that it has been in many a long year. . . .

The volunteer movement caught on in great style here in Dublin. Such an outpouring of young fellows was never seen. They filled the Rink in the Rotunda Gardens (which holds 7,000), filled the adjacent garden, overflowed into the Concert Hall . . . and packed the streets around the entrances. . . . 'Tis good to be in Ireland these times.

. . . Hundreds of young fellows who would not be interested in the National Movement, even on the milk and water side are in these volunteers and are saying things which proves that the right spot has been touched in them by the volunteering. Wait till they get their fist clutching the steel barrel of a business rifle and then Irish instincts and Irish manhood can be relied upon.

—Tom Clarke, letter to Joe McGarrity[14]

top left: Eoin MacNeill.

top right: Bulmer Hobson.

left: Young members of Na Fianna Éireann, 1914.

above: Report of the founding of the Irish Volunteers, *Irish Times*, November 26, 1913.

Belgian Congo disgusted him. Casement's report on the appalling human rights violations he had witnessed received massive publicity in Europe and America and forced Leopold of Belgium to make concessions. Casement had long been an Irish nationalist. He was a Gaelic Leaguer and wrote articles for the nationalist press under the pen name Sean Bhean Bhocht. But unlike other Irishmen who worked for the empire, Casement saw very clear parallels between the effects of colonialism in Africa and the historical situation of Ireland. Casement moved from Africa to South America, where he again exposed the dark underbelly of colonial exploitation, this time the dreadful treatment of the indigenous Putamayo Indians in Brazil at the hands of the rubber barons. In 1911 Roger Casement was knighted by the British government for his services to human rights. It was an honor that would have severe repercussions for this increasingly militant nationalist.

As the Irish Volunteers gathered momentum throughout the country, John Redmond and the Irish Party took note. Anxious to retain control of nationalist Ireland, Redmond quickly ensured that he was appointed to the executive committee of the Irish Volunteers. The Volunteers constituted a very broad church indeed.

Like their unionist counterparts in Ulster, nationalist women also mobilized. A few months after the meeting in the Rotunda, another public meet-

It was only because I was an Irishman that I could understand *fully*, I think, the whole scheme of wrongdoing at work here in the Congo.

It is a tyranny beyond conception, save only perhaps, to an Irish mind alive to the horrors once daily enacted in this land.

—Roger Casement, letters to Alice Stopford Green and William Cadbury

ing was held, this time to organize the women activists. The new organization was called Cumann na mBan, the women's branch of the Irish Volunteers.

As Ireland became increasingly agitated about its constitutional future, conditions for the poor and working class of Dublin in the first decades of the twentieth century continued to be shameful. The Georgian former townhouses of the Ascendancy who had decamped to London following the Act of Union had long become squalid tenements lacking water and sanitary facilities. Living conditions for the poor were appalling, and their mortality rates were among the worst in the British Isles.

Unlike Belfast, which had benefited considerably from the Industrial Revolution, Dublin had made its wealth on commercial activities and lacked the skilled workers necessary for an industrial base. Most Dublin workers were unskilled or general workers and relied on casual labor. The nascent labor movement under James Larkin

opposite left: Group of slaves in the Belgian Congo, 1905.

opposite right: Roger Casement.

Group photograph of Cumann na mBan.

and the recently returned James Connolly found fertile ground.

On August 26, 1913, over twenty thousand Dublin workers under the leadership of Larkin and Connolly had gone on strike for better conditions and for the right to organize in trade unions. The employers, under their leader William Martin Murphy, reacted to the strike by locking out their workers.

Murphy in many ways typified the new growing Catholic bourgeoisie. He was a nationalist insofar as he supported Home Rule and had been a former Irish Parliamentary Party MP. He had many commercial interests and owned a number of newspapers, the *Irish Independent* and the *Irish Catholic* among them.

The 1913 Lockout, as it became known, was an intensely bitter and long-drawn-out dispute. Soup kitchens were set up to feed the starving children of the strikers by Countess Markievicz, Helena Moloney, and other radical activists. Police and workers clashed violently on the streets. Connolly accused the police of brutality and of being stooges of the employers. By January 1914, the workers, unable to feed their families, finally bowed to the inevitable and gave in.

In response to the violent clashes, James Connolly had organized a group of workers into a small private army. The Irish Citizen Army (ICA) had some two hundred members. Connolly was an ardent supporter of women's rights, and among the people he appointed to leadership positions in

the Citizen Army was Countess Markievicz. Formerly Constance Gore-Booth, before she married a Polish count, she came from a Protestant Anglo-Irish Ascendancy background. She had long been prominent in radical and nationalist circles and had been involved in forming Na Fianna Éireann, the youth wing of the separatist movement. She was also prominently involved in Cumann na mBan. Other women prominent in the ICA were Dr. Kathleen Lynn, Helena Moloney, and Marie Perolz, all of whom would later take an active part in the 1916 rebellion.

The Irish Citizen Army would remain in existence after the strike had ended, continuing to drill and train. They were another small but important addition to the increasing militarization of Ireland.

Encouragement for the physical force republican tradition continued to come from America. Clan na Gael, in addition to providing moral

Baton charge by police during the Dublin Lockout of 1913.

support and financial assistance, increasingly hosted visits by leading Irish separatists, including Pádraig Pearse. Although he had spoken on Home Rule platforms in the past, Pearse was now being drawn to the physical force tradition. Despite the misgivings of some, he had been recruited into the IRB by Tom Clarke. In 1914 Pádraig Pearse went to the United States on a lecture tour organized by Clan na Gael ostensibly to raise funds for his school, St Enda's. In America, he met Devoy, addressed public meetings, and perfected his rhetorical and oratorical skills. By the time he returned to Dublin, he was fully committed to armed rebellion.

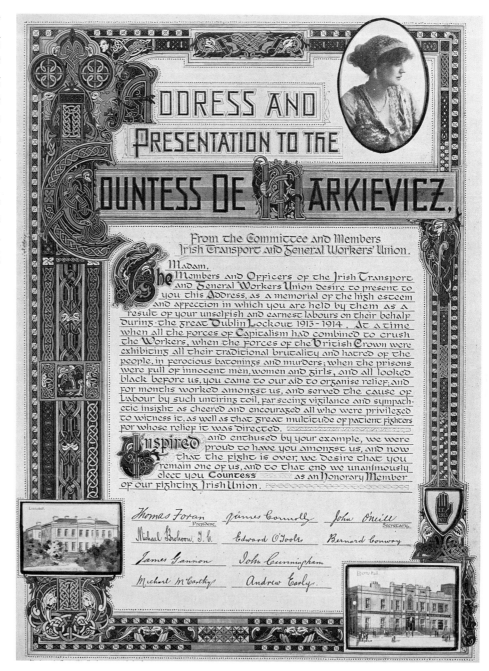

Image of the presentation to Countess Markievicz from the Irish Transport and General Workers Union for her services during the 1913 Lockout.

1778 — — CELEBRATION — — 1914
of the 136th Anniversary of the Birth of
=:= ROBERT EMMET =:=
— by the —
CLAN-NA-GAEL OF LONG ISLAND
At The Brooklyn Academy of Music
Lafayette Avenue, Brooklyn, N. Y.
On Sunday Eve'g, March 1st, 1914, At 8:15 o'clock

HON. CHARLES S. DEVOY | Address: "Robert Emmet" by
Will Preside | GOV MARTIN H. GLYNN
Address— "Present-day Conditions in Ireland," by
P. H. PEARSE.

Vocal and Instrumental Irish Music by Eminent Artists.
Concert of Irish Popular Airs at 7:30   Doors Open 7:15 o'clock
TICKETS,   -   -   -   25 CENTS EACH
All Seats are Reserved, Prices 25c., 50., 75.

Advertisement in the *Gaelic American*,
February 28, 1914, p. 8.

To the grey haired men whom I see on this platform, to John Devoy and Richard Burke, I bring, then, this message from Ireland; that their seed sowing of forty years ago has not been without its harvest, that there are young men and boys in Ireland who remember what they were taught, and who with God's blessing, will one day take, or make an opportunity of putting their teaching into practice.

— Pádraig Pearse, speaking at the Emmet Celebration organized by Clan na Gael in Brooklyn, March 1, 1914[15]

What need I say but that today Ireland is turning her face once more to the old path? Nothing seems more definitely to emerge when one looks at the movements that are stirring both above the surface and beneath the surface in mens' minds at home than the fact that the new generation is reaffirming the Fenian faith, the faith of Emmet. . . . I cannot speak for the Volunteers; I am not authorized to say when they will use their arms or where or how. I can speak only for myself; and it is strictly a personal perception that I am recording, but a perception that to me is very clear, when I say that before this generation has passed, the Volunteers will draw the sword of Ireland. There is no truth but the old truth and no way but the old way. Home Rule may come or may not come, but under Home Rule or its absence there remains for the Volunteers and for Ireland the substantial business of achieving Irish nationhood. And I do not know how nationhood is achieved except by armed men. I do not know how nationhood is guarded except by armed men.

—Pádraig Pearse, addressing Irish Americans in New York, March 2, 1914[16]

War Clouds Gather

In the North, preparations for a coup d'etat were gaining momentum. By spring 1914 the Ulster Volunteer Force could mobilize some 60,000 men. On the night of April 24, nearly 25,000 rifles and 3 to 5 million rounds of ammunition were landed by the Ulster Volunteer Force at three locations on the Ulster coast: Larne, Bangor, and Donaghadee. The gunrunning had been carried out with the support and knowledge of Craig and Carson. No government action was taken.

The Irish Volunteers continued to drill and march, but they were hampered by a severe lack of weapons. A very important development occurred when John Redmond managed to seize control of the Volunteer ruling executive council. The differences between the Redmondite faction and the

I walked up and down the deck tormented by the thought of all those men waiting for me to bring them the weapons with which to fight for their religion, their liberty and all that was dear to them....I went into my cabin and threw myself on my knees, and in simple language told God all about it: what this meant to Ulster, that there was nothing sordid in what we desired, that we wanted nothing selfishly. I pointed out all this to God, and thought of the old Psalm 'O God our help in ages past, our hope for years to come'.

—Major M. H. Crawford, organizer of the Larne gunrunning[17]

Unloading arms from the *Asgard* at Howth pier.

opposite: Report in the *Irish Independent* on the aftermath of the Bachelor's Walk killings of civilians.

radicals were clear to see. Although members of the IRB were furious, hoping to control the Volunteers and move them in the direction of armed insurrection and revolution, Redmond was for the moment happy to have the Volunteer movement behind him to strengthen his hand at Westminster.

Although the Home Rule Bill had passed, it was not yet on the Statute books. It also importantly included in its provision an opt-out clause for a period of six years. This was already pointing in the direction of partition, though whether four, six, or nine counties were to be excluded from the provision of Home Rule was yet to be decided. A conference held by George V attempted to resolve the issue but ended in failure.

The "Irish Question," however, was driven from the headlines by the tribulations of the Austro-Hungarian Empire. As the prime minister was reporting to his cabinet on the failure of the Irish conference, the danger of impending crisis in Europe was magnifying. For those in Ireland, however, their own affairs continued to take precedence.

Prompted by the success of the Ulster Volunteer Force in landing arms at Larne, supporters of the Irish Volunteers attempted the same. Two days later, on April 26, the *Asgard* sailed into Howth Harbor with a cargo of nine hundred rifles. Eight hundred Irish Volunteers marched from Dublin city center to take possession of the weapons. As the Volunteers reached the city with the arms, they were stopped by a company of the King's Own Scottish Borderers. The Volunteers

refused to give up their weapons, leading to a few fistfights, and they managed to get away with the rifles. As the soldiers were returning empty-handed to barracks there was a crowd waiting at Bachelor's Walk. Some stones were thrown and "the soldiers opened fire. Four civilians were killed. Nationalist opinion was outraged. There were, it seemed, different standards for unionist orange and nationalist green.

Huge numbers of people lined the streets as members of the Irish Volunteers and the Irish Citizen Army, many armed with the guns, landed in Howth accompanying the coffins of those killed in the confrontation. Attitudes had hardened on all sides. Ireland appeared to stand on the brink of open civil war.

The discussion [on Ireland] had reached its inconclusive end, and the Cabinet was about to separate, when the quiet grave tones of Sir Edward Grey's voice were heard reading a document which had just been brought to him from the Foreign Office. It was the Austrian note to Serbia. He had been reading or speaking for several minutes before I could disengage my mind from the tedious and bewildering debate which had just closed. We were all very tired, but gradually as the phrases and sentences followed one another, impressions of a wholly different character began to form in my mind. This note was clearly an ultimatum; but it was an ultimatum such as had never been penned in modern times. As the reading proceeded, it seemed absolutely impossible that any State in the world could accept it, or that any acceptance, however abject, would satisfy the aggressor. The parishes of Fermanagh and Tyrone faded back into the mists and squalls of Ireland, and a strange light began immediately, but by perceptible gradations, to fall and grow upon the map of Europe.
—Winston Churchill[18]

opposite: Funeral cortege for the victims of Bachelor's Walk passes by the GPO.

John Redmond and members of the National Volunteers.

The Great War

Unrelated events, however, were overtaking Ireland. On August 3, 1914, Germany invaded Belgium. The British foreign secretary rose in Westminster and declared war on Germany. The war that Tom Clarke and the IRB had been long prophesying and eagerly awaiting had come to pass. The Great War had begun. Nothing in Europe or in Ireland would ever be the same.

In Westminster the Home Rule Bill was passed only to be shelved for the duration of the war. Most of the Ulster Volunteer Force joined the British Army en masse out of loyalty and duty to the British Empire. John Redmond, hopeful of a speedy implementation of Home Rule after the war, immediately offered the support of the Irish Volunteers and called on them to enlist in the British Army. Many thousands answered his call. Others were horrified. The Volunteers split, with a small minority following Eoin MacNeill, Pearse, and the more militant members. The vast majority remained loyal to Redmond and were now known as the Irish National Volunteers. The contradictions and schisms in Irish nationalism were becoming apparent. Although Arthur Griffith and the Volunteers under MacNeill argued strongly that Ireland had no business fighting a war with

ENGLAND DECLARES WAR AGAINST GERMANY.

MOMENTOUS BRITISH DECISION.

UNSATISFACTORY REPLY TO ULTIMATUM

GERMANY DECLARES WAR ON FRANCE & BELGIUM.

INVASION OF BELGIAN NEUTRALITY.

A BRITISH MINE-LAYING VESSEL SUNK IN THE GERMAN OCEAN.

KAISER'S WARLIKE THRONE SPEECH

FRENCH PRESIDENT'S MESSAGE CAUSES FRANTIC ENTHUSIASM IN THE CHAMBER.

THE BRINK OF DEVASTATING CARNAGE.

TEXT OF BRITISH DECLARATION AGAINST GERMANY.

OFFICIAL GOVERNMENT STATEMENT.

GERMANY.

THE KAISER GRASPS THE SWORD.

NO PARTIES NOW—ONLY GERMANS.

APPEAL IN SPEECH FROM THE THRONE.

RUSSIA.

RUSSIAN SEAPORT BOMBARDED.

MAP OF THE FRONTIERS.

The lamps are going out all over Europe; we shall not see them lit again in our lifetime.

—Lord Grey, British Foreign Secretary, August 3, 1914[19]

COME & JOIN THIS HAPPY THRONG

OFF TO THE FRONT

The interests of Ireland—of the whole of Ireland—are at stake in this war. This war is undertaken in the defense of the highest principles of religion and morality and right, and it would be a disgrace for ever to our country and a reproach to her manhood and a denial of the lessons of her history if young Ireland confined their efforts to remaining at home to defend the shores of Ireland from an unlikely invasion, and to shrinking from the duty of proving on the field of battle that gallantry and courage which has distinguished our race all through its history. I say to you, therefore, your duty is twofold. I am glad to see such magnificent material for soldiers around me, and I say to you: "Go on drilling and make yourself efficient for the Work, and then account yourselves as men, not only for Ireland itself, but wherever the fighting line extends, in defense of right, of freedom, and religion in this war."

—John Redmond, addressing volunteers at Woodenbridge, County Wicklow, September 20, 1914

Ireland is not at war with Germany. She has no quarrel with any continental power. England is at war with Germany, and Mr. Redmond has offered England the services of the National Volunteers to defend Ireland. What has Ireland to defend, and whom has she to defend it against? Has she a native Constitution or a national Government to defend? All know that she has not. All know that both were wrested from her by the power to whom Mr. Redmond offers the services of National Ireland. All know that Mr. Redmond has made his offer without receiving a quid pro quo. There is no European Power waging war against the people of Ireland. There are two European Powers at war with the people who dominate Ireland from Dublin Castle. The call to the Volunteers to 'defend Ireland' is a call to them to defend the bureaucracy entrenched in that edifice.

—Arthur Griffith, September 1914[20]

I found myself in a camp of four thousand men where . . . everybody thought exactly alike; Protestant fervour was at its height . . . the tents were decorated, many of them, with Union Jacks and Orange emblems and at night the overflowing enthusiasm of the men found its outlet in song. For the first week or so I went to sleep to the strains of Orange ditties such as:

Come back to Ireland those who are
    over the sea
come back to Ireland and fight for
    liberty
They are flying the flag, the harp
    without a crown
So come back to Ireland and keep
    popery down.

—J. L. Stewart-Moore, Trinity College student and member of the Royal Irish Rifles[21]

opposite: The *Irish Independent* announces England's declaration of war against Germany.

Irish infantrymen off to World War I, 1915.

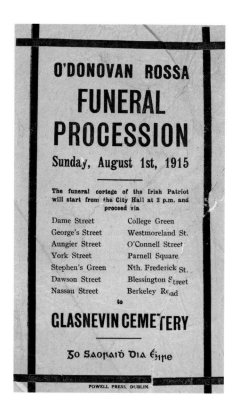

Germany, many thousands of recruits answered Redmond's call. They believed that they were defending the right of small nations and that Ireland would receive Home Rule after the war. The Ulster Volunteers were also clear in their motivation: they were, once again, defending king and country and also hoped for a reward for their loyalty at war's end. It was a circle that would be impossible to square.

While thousands of Irishmen followed Redmond's call to fight for Ireland by enlisting in the British Army, the IRB, strongly backed by Devoy and Clan na Gael in America, were plotting their moves. For them, the war was an opportunity not to be missed. They were ready to strike in armed insurrection and planned to do so before the war was over.

The IRB had by now managed to infiltrate themselves into every group active in Irish nationalism, including the Irish Volunteers. When the old Fenian and mastermind of the dynamite campaign against Britain, Jeremiah O'Donovan Rossa, died in New York in 1915, Clan na Gael and the IRB decided to bring his body back to Dublin for burial in Glasnevin Cemetery. It would be an opportunity for Irish militant nationalism to show its power in a public display. In a move "surprising many, Tom Clarke chose Pádraig Pearse to give the funeral oration. It was a clear acknowledgement of Pearse's growing importance as a public figure within militant circles.

Standing at Rossa's graveside, Pearse addressed the large crowd, many of them dressed in full Irish Volunteer uniform. His historic words

left: Pearse (to the right of priest) waits to give the oration at the graveside of O'Donovan Rossa.

right: Funeral procession program for Jeremiah O'Donovan Rossa.

Funeral Oration for Jeremiah O'Donovan Rossa

It has seemed right, before we turn away from this place in which we have laid the mortal remains of O'Donovan Rossa, that one among us should, in the name of all, speak the praise of that valiant man, and endeavor to formulate the thought and the hope that are in us as we stand around his grave. And if there is anything that makes it fitting that I, rather than some other, rather than one of the grey-haired men who were young with him and shared in his labour and in his suffering, should speak here, it is perhaps that I may be taken as speaking on behalf of a new generation that has been re-baptized in the Fenian faith, and that has accepted the responsibility of carrying out the Fenian programme. I propose to you then that, here by the grave of this unrepentant Fenian, we renew our baptismal vows; that, here by the grave of this uncon-quered and unconquerable man, we ask of God, each one for himself, such unshakable purpose, such high and gallant courage, such unbreakable strength of soul as belonged to O'Donovan Rossa.

Deliberately here we avow our-selves, as he avowed himself in the dock, Irishmen of one allegiance only. We of the Irish Volunteers, and you others who are associated with us in today's task and duty, are bound to-gether and must stand together henceforth in brotherly union for the achievement of the freedom of Ire-land. And we know only one defini-tion of freedom: it is Tone's definition, it is Mitchel's definition, it is Rossa's definition. Let no man blaspheme the cause that the dead generations of Ireland served by giving it any other name and definition than their name and their definition.

We stand at Rossa's grave not in sadness but rather in exaltation of spirit that has been given to us to come thus into so close a commu-nion with that brave and splendid Gael. Splendid and holy causes are served by men who are themselves splendid and holy. O'Donovan Rossa was splendid in the proud manhood of him, splendid in the heroic grace of him, splendid in the Gaelic strength and clarity and truth of him. And all that splendor and pride and strength was compatible with a humility and a simplicity of devotion to Ireland, to all that was olden and beautiful and Gaelic in Ireland, the holiness and simplicity of patriotism of a Michael O'Clery or of an Eoghan O'Growney. The clear true eyes of this man almost alone in his day vi-sioned Ireland as we of today would surely have her: not free merely, but Gaelic as well; not Gaelic merely, but free as well.

In a closer spiritual communion with him now than ever before or perhaps ever again, in a spiritual com-munion with those of his day, living and dead, who suffered with him in English prisons, in communion of spirit too with our own dear com-rades who suffer in English prisons today, and speaking on their behalf as well as our own, we pledge to Ireland our love, and we pledge to English rule in Ireland our hate. This is a place of peace, sacred to the dead, where men should speak with all charity and with all restraint; but I hold it a Christian thing, as O'Donovan Rossa held it, to hate evil, to hate untruth, to hate oppression, and hating them, to strive to overthrow them.

Our foes are strong and wise and wary but, strong and wise and wary as they are, they cannot undo the miracles of God who ripens in the hearts of young men the seeds sown by the young men of a former gen-eration. And the seeds sown by the young men of '65 and '67 are coming to their miraculous ripening today. Rulers and Defenders of Realms had need to be wary if they would guard against such processes. Life springs from death; and from the graves of patriot men and women spring living nations. The defenders of this Realm have worked well in secret and in the open. They think that they have paci-fied Ireland. They think that they have purchased half of us and intimidated the other half. They think that they have foreseen everything, think that they have provided against every-thing; but the fools, the fools, the fools! —they have left us our Fenian dead, and while Ireland holds these graves, Ireland unfree shall never be at peace.

—Pádraig Pearse, Glasnevin Cemetery, August 1915

Members of the ICA parade outside Croydon Park, Dublin, 1915.

were a clear signal of what was to come. Within weeks of the beginning of the First World War, Clan na Gael in America had opened lines of communication with the German embassy in New York. Roger Casement, by now in the inner circle, was sent to Germany as the main envoy. Casement traveled to Germany from New York by a circuitous route, avoiding an assassination attempt by British intelligence on the way

Casement's sojourn in Berlin was not a happy one. His attempts to recruit an Irish Brigade from captured Irish POWs failed dismally, and he was making little headway in convincing the German military authorities to send men and weapons to Ireland.

Meantime, the war, which was confidently predicted to have been over by the previous Christmas, continued to drag on with increasing casualties. The IRB and their American allies in Clan na Gael, anxious to act before war's end, continued to plot. In April, Joseph Mary Plunkett traveled to Germany to meet with Casement. At the end of May 1915 a small group, Pearse, Plunkett, and Éamonn Ceannt, were appointed by the IRB to oversee preparations for a rising. This "military committee," as it was known, was later expanded to include Clarke and Mac Diarmada. (It would later include Connolly and MacDonagh, the so-called seven-man military council). This was a conspiracy within a conspiracy. Eoin MacNeill, although nominally still head of the Volunteers, was not privy to their plans.

This small group continued their preparations in great secrecy throughout the rest of 1915 and into 1916. They were not the only group intent on a rising. James Connolly and his small Irish Citizen Army were becoming more vociferous in calling for a revolutionary insurrection. In January 1916, afraid of a precipitous move by the ICA, the military council of the IRB invited Connolly into the inner circle.

He agreed, and together they decided on a joint rising timed for Easter, a date whose symbolic significance was not lost on the more religiously minded of the rebels, such as Pearse and Plunkett. The rising was to be held under the guise of maneuvers by the Volunteers, a habitual activity, and one to which both the authorities and the general population were becoming inured. The leaders of the Volunteers no longer in the inner circle, including Eoin MacNeill and Bulmer Hobson, were to be kept ignorant of the real purpose behind the mobilization. On St. Patrick's Day 1916 a trial run took place. Some 1,400 volunteers took control of Dublin city center for over an hour, with a further 4,500 mobilized outside the capital. The clock was now ticking.

Roger Casement and John Devoy in the U.S. before Casement's departure for Germany.

On April 3, with word received that arms were on their way from Germany, Pearse issued orders for large-scale maneuvers of the Volunteers to take place on Easter Sunday. Although Dublin Castle was in receipt of intelligence concerning an imminent rebellion, the authorities failed to act.

Casement, having failed in his attempts to enlist full German military support for an Irish rising, did finally manage to secure a shipment of arms, some twenty thousand rifles, ten machine guns, and a substantial amount of ammunition. This cargo left Lubeck on the *Aud* on April 9, bound for the Irish coast. Casement, bitterly disappointed with the level of German aid, followed two days later onboard a submarine. They intended to rendezvous with the *Aud* and its cargo off the Kerry coast in time for Easter. Although nothing like the military force that Casement had originally hoped for, the successful landing of the shipment would provide enough arms for a countrywide insurrection with a good chance of at least holding out for a considerable time. The wheels had been put in motion.

In Dublin, preparations were reaching fever pitch among the conspirators. Pearse's order for general maneuvers of the Volunteers for Easter Sunday had been received throughout the country. It was now Holy Thursday, April 20.

The *Aud*, which carried German arms for the Rising.

Holy Thursday, April 20

Bulmer Hobson, the secretary of the Irish Volunteers who, along with MacNeill, had also been left in the dark about the planned rising, was informed that an armed insurrection was planned and that Volunteer units throughout the country had received orders to take part under

Casement on the U-19 submarine setting off for Ireland. He had shaved his beard in an effort to remain incognito.

cover of the maneuvers. Hobson immediately went to MacNeill's house and, rousing him from bed, told him of the plans for the rising. MacNeill was thunderstruck and, outraged at what he felt was Pearse's duplicity, went immediately to confront him. MacNeill told Pearse that he would do all in his power to prevent a rising short of informing Dublin Castle. He would not allow "a half armed force to be called out," asserting that there would be "no waste of lives for which I am directly responsible." MacNeill's reaction caused consternation among the conspirators. Later that day MacNeill agreed to meet with Seán Mac Diarmada. Mac Diarmada informed him of the imminent arrival of German arms. In the light of this news, MacNeill was reluctantly persuaded to go along with the plans. His support, however, was to be short-lived.

That same day the *Aud*, having completed her perilous journey, was making her way through the waters of Tralee Bay. She dropped anchor at the designated spot in the late afternoon. The pre-arranged signal was not answered. Unknown to both sides, confusion had arisen as to the date the arms were due. The IRB's military council had earlier sent Joseph Mary Plunkett's sister, Philomena, to New York with a urgent message for John Devoy. Devoy was asked to forward it to the *Aud*, requesting that they delay the landings until Easter Sunday in case an early arrival would alert the British. He passed on the message to the Germans, but the *Aud* carried no radio and never received the message. It was another indication of the quagmire of chaos and confusion that would bedevil the conspirators' plans.

Good Friday, April 21

Just after midnight the submarine carrying Casement was in Tralee Bay only a mile northwest of the *Aud*. The ships missed each other. With no sign of the *Aud*, Casement and two companions set out under cover of dark in a collapsible dinghy, hoping to rendezvous with local Irish Volunteers. The boat capsized in the heavy surf. Casement barely made it to shore. The boat was found early that morning at Banna Strand along with three revolvers and one thousand rounds of ammunition. Casement, who had nearly died from hypothermia in the cold waters, was arrested later that morning by local police from the Royal Irish Constabulary (RIC) and was taken to Tralee, the beginning of a journey that would lead him inexorably to the scaffold.

The litany of mishaps and disasters was not yet over. That afternoon the *Aud* was intercepted by British warships as it fruitlessly sailed up and down Tralee Bay. As the *Aud* was escorted to Queenstown under armed guard, the captain decided to scuttle his ship to prevent his cargo falling into English hands. The twenty thousand rifles destined for the Irish Volunteers sank to the bottom of Cork Harbor.

That same evening a group of five Volunteers, including a wireless operator sent by Mac Diarmada to set up a transmitter to communicate with the German ships, had arrived in Kerry. On their way out of Killorglin, the second car missed a turn on the narrow twisting roads. The car plunged off Ballykissane Pier and into the waters of Castlemaine Harbor. Three of the Volunteers, including the wireless specialist, drowned. On the back seat of the car was the signal lamp with which they intended to signal the *Aud*. It was now Easter Saturday, April 22.

Report of Casement's capture in the *Ulster Herald*.

Easter Saturday, April 22

News of Casement's arrest and the loss of the arms had by now trickled through to the military council in Dublin. They were despondent but determined to continue with their plans. At Liberty Hall, members of the Irish Citizen Army gathered their weapons and made final preparations.

MacNeill, learning of the disasters in Kerry, was adamant that Sunday's maneuvers must be called off and made a final desperate effort to abort the rising. He sent trusted couriers with handwritten notes throughout the country countermanding Pearse's mobilization orders. One of those who went was Michael Joseph O'Rahilly, known as "The O'Rahilly," one of MacNeill's right-hand men who played an important part in later events.

MacNeill's last act of the day was to deliver the countermanding order for publication in the following day's *Sunday Independent*: "Owing to the very critical position, all orders given to Irish Volunteers for tomorrow, Easter Sunday, are hereby rescinded, and no parades, marches, or other movement of Irish Volunteers will take place. Each individual Volunteer will obey this order strictly in every particular." The countermanding order was the final blow to the plans for a successful rising. Whatever faint chance of military success they might have had at full strength had evaporated with MacNeill's order and the loss of the arms shipment. With the British alerted by the capture of Casement and the *Aud* and the leaking of an intelligence document from Dublin Castle, the leaders knew a crackdown was imminent.

As Easter Sunday morning dawned, Pearse, Clarke, MacDonagh, Plunkett, Ceannt, Mac Diarmada, and Connolly, the leaders of the conspirators, realized the plans they had carefully laid were in tatters. But not to fight would be a disaster much greater than a military defeat. The more romantic among them, such as Pearse, saw the possibility of self-sacrifice to redeem Ireland's honor and to pass the torch on to a new generation. The more pragmatic felt that at the very least it might win Ireland a place at the peace talks at the end of the war. As the rebel leaders, the military council, made their way into Liberty Hall for one final meeting, the fate of Ireland, and their own fates, still hung in the balance. The die, however, would soon be cast.

Sunday Independent, Easter Sunday, April 23, 1916, carrying MacNeill's countermand and reporting on events in Kerry.

PART TWO

Insurrection

Easter Sunday, April 23

DUBLIN AWOKE TO A BRIGHT MORN-
ing, but the good weather did nothing
to lift the spirits of the rebel leaders as
they made their way to Liberty Hall for
an emergency meeting of the military
council. For months they had plotted
and planned for this day, the day when
Ireland would rise, but now all their
plans seemed in ruins. Confusion and
disappointment reigned in the rebel
ranks.

As the council continued to debate, Eoin MacNeill made another last-
ditch effort to stop any mobilization of
the Irish Volunteers, sending a personal
letter to Éamon de Valera. MacNeill's
words fell on deaf ears. During a highly
charged meeting, the council decided
to postpone the Rising until noon the
following day, Easter Monday, despite
Clarke's insistence that they proceed
there and then.

That evening, Liberty Hall was
a hive of activity. James Connolly addressed the assembled members of the
Irish Citizen Army with fighting words.

Letter from Eoin MacNeill to
Éamon de Valera, Easter Sunday, 1916.

Copies of the Proclamation of the Irish Republic were hurriedly printed to be signed by the seven members of the military council, who had now designated themselves the Provisional Government of the Irish Republic. Tom Clarke was given the honor of being the first to sign. The other signatories were Pádraig Pearse, Thomas MacDonagh, Joseph Mary Plunkett, Éamonn Ceannt, Seán Mac Diarmada, and James Connolly.

As the rebels openly gathered at Liberty Hall, the British authorities were in a state of some confusion. They had been lulled into a false sense of security by the sinking of the *Aud* and the capture of Casement. Remarkably, British policy towards the Irish Volunteers during wartime had been one of containment rather than open suppression, as espoused and practiced by Britain's two most senior officials in Ireland, Chief Secretary Augustine Birrell and Under-Secretary Sir Matthew Nathan. Learning about the *Aud* and MacNeill's intervention, Birrell left for London, leaving Nathan in charge.

Nathan spent the day at Dublin Castle convening meetings with his military advisors. Late

I saw Eoin MacNeill's countermanding order in the paper and heard the discussion in Liberty Hall. Connolly was there. They were all heartbroken, and when they were not crying they were cursing. I kept thinking, "Does this mean that we are not going out?" There were thousands like us. It was foolish of MacNeill and those to think they could call it off. They could not. Many of us thought we would go out single-handed, if necessary.

The Easter Sunday was a day of confusion, excitement and disappointment in Liberty Hall. I stayed there all day and all night. There was a lot of work to be done preparing food upstairs for the men who came from different parts of the city and had brought no rations. . . . Dr. Lynn went home, but Jinny Shanahan and I slept again on the overcoats in the room behind the shop.

—Helena Moloney, witness statement[2]

left: Augustine Birrell.

right: Sir Matthew Nathan.

that night he called a conference at the Vice-Regal Lodge in the Phoenix Park. In attendance were Nathan himself and the Viceroy Lord Wimborne, together with the Commissioner of the Dublin Metropolitan Police and senior Army staff officers. They were informed that intelligence indicated that explosives had been smuggled into Liberty Hall. They discussed launching an immediate military raid on Liberty Hall and a swoop on Volunteer leaders. At 11:30 pm the meeting ended. Nathan and Wimborne had decided to wait until they heard from Birrell before ordering arrests. That delay would have momentous consequences.

I stayed around the hall all day. I should say it was about four p.m. when the Citizen Army, with their arms, bandoliers and rifles on a cart, started gathering outside. Crowds seemed to gather, as if they were waiting and expecting something. They were all gathered around the Hall and over at the Custom House arch. They were watching the place all day long, as if waiting to hear something....

The Citizen Army men all knew they were definitely in for a fight, and, naturally, their families—they were all terribly loyal and a terribly compact body.... Women and girls came over, and kissed them and gave them packages, cigarettes and things.
—Nora (Connolly) O'Brien, eldest daughter of James Connolly, describing the Liberty Hall meeting on Easter Sunday[3]

opposite: The Vice-Regal Lodge in the Phoenix Park, Dublin, home to the Viceroy, Lord Wimborne, and his family.

The Viceroy, Lord Wimborne.

"You are now under arms," he concluded. "You will not lay down your arms until you have struck a blow for Ireland!"

The men cheered, shots were fired into the air, and that night their barracks was Liberty Hall.

You might think a demonstration of this character, a speech in the open, would attract enough attention from the police to make them send a report to the authorities. None was sent. They had come to feel, I suppose, that while there was so much talk there would be little action. Nor did they remember that Easter is always the anniversary of that fight hundreds of years ago when native Irish came to drive the foreigner from Dublin. This year, in addition, it fell upon the date of the Battle of Clontarf, so there was double reason for sentiment to seize upon the day for the revolt.

During the night, Irishmen from England and Scotland who had been encamped at Kimmage with some others, came into Dublin and joined the men at Liberty Hall. Next morning I saw them while they were drawn up, waiting for orders.
—Margaret Skinnider, ICA volunteer, describing Connolly's address at Liberty Hall on Easter Sunday[4]

Easter Monday, April 24

A WARM AND SUNNY DAY. FEW DUBLINERS knew what lay in store. Some, however, were only too aware of what lay ahead. By 10:00 am the military council and members of the Irish Citizen Army had begun to muster at Liberty Hall. The building was adorned with a banner proclaiming "We serve neither King nor Kaiser but Ireland."

At the same time as the rebels were mustering at Liberty Hall, a serious and rather somber Nathan arrived at Dublin Castle. He was joined shortly afterwards by Major Ivor Price, a former RIC county inspector who was now the chief military intelligence officer.

Shortly before 12:00 noon, the hour designated for the start of the Rising, the four Volunteer

It was on Easter Morning the boys
    got the call
To join their battalions in park, glen
    and hall,
In less than an hour they were out on
    parade;
They were true men tho' few in the
    Dublin Brigade.

—contemporary ballad[5]

Liberty Hall before the Rising.

The General Post Office (GPO) and Sackville Street just before the Rising.

Thomas Clarke.

Edward (Ned) Daly.

Margaret Skinnider.

Éamon de Valera in Volunteer uniform, 1916.

Countess Markievicz in ICA uniform.

Seán Connolly.

Michael Mallin.

Éamonn Ceannt.

battalions in Dublin gathered and prepared to occupy strategic positions. Due to MacNeill's countermand, they were at nothing like full strength. All told, some two thousand men and women of the Irish Volunteers, Cumann na mBan, Na Fianna Éireann, and the Irish Citizen Army assembled at various locations throughout the capital.

As the rebels gathered and the castle pondered, the citizens of Dublin, still oblivious to events unfolding around them, were enjoying the Easter holiday. Many of them, including most of the officers of the British garrisons in the city, made their way to the races at nearby Fairyhouse. At their various locations, the rebels waited as the 12:00 deadline approached. Scouts were sent out from Liberty Hall to check on troop movements in and around the capital

Shortly before noon, Pearse and Connolly, at the head of a column of 150 men and women drawn from the ranks of the Volunteers, Cumann na mBan, and the ICA, left Liberty Hall, making their way to the General Post Office (GPO) in nearby Sackville Street (now O'Connell Street) on Dublin's main thoroughfare. The GPO had been designated as the main garrison of rebel forces and headquarters of the provisional government. Their strength was a fraction of what they had planned for it to be.

Rebels inside the GPO.

On Easter Monday morning there was a great hosting of armed and disciplined men at Liberty Hall. Padraic Pearse and James Connolly addressed us and told us that from now the Volunteers and the I.C.A. were not two forces, but the wings of the Irish Republican Army.

There were a considerable number of I.C.A. women. These were absolutely on the same footing as the men.

—Countess Markievicz[7]

I was sent on my bicycle to scout about the city and report if troops from any of the barracks were stirring. They were not. Moreover, I learned that their officers, for the most part, were off to the races at [Fairyhouse] in the gayest of moods.

When I returned to report to Mr. Connolly, I had my first glimpse of Padraic Pearse, provisional president of the Irish Republic. He was a tall man, over six feet, with broad shoulders slightly stooped from long hours as a student and writer. But he had a soldierly bearing and was very cool and determined, I thought, for a man on whom so much responsibility rested—at the very moment, too, when his dream was about to take form. Thomas McDonagh was also there. I had not seen him before in uniform, and he, too, gave me the impression that our Irish scholars must be soldiers at bottom, so well did he appear in his green uniform.

—Margaret Skinnider[8]

As the order 'By the left, quick march' was given, a rousing cheer rang out from the rather imposing crowd who had by then gathered in front of Liberty Hall. We moved off at a brisk pace, swung left into Lower Abbey Street, and headed up towards O'Connell Street. We had, for good or ill, set out on a great adventure.

—Commandant William James Brennan-Whitmore, Irish Volunteer[9]

I was next detailed as dispatch rider for the St. Stephen's Green Command. Again I went out to scout, this time for Commandant Mallin. If I did not find the military moving, I was to remain at the end of the Green until I should see our men coming in to take possession. There were no soldiers in sight; only a policeman standing at the far end of the Green doing nothing. He paid no attention to me; I was only a girl on a bicycle.... [He] was the last policeman I saw until after the rising was over. They seemed to vanish from the streets of Dublin.

It was a great moment for me, as I stood there, when ... I caught sight of men in dark green uniforms coming along in twos and threes to take up their position in and about the Green and at the corners of the streets leading in to it....

At last all the men were standing ready, awaiting the signal. In every part of Dublin similar small groups were waiting for the hour to strike. The revolution had begun!

—Margaret Skinnider[10]

top left: Dublin Castle gate, ca. 1916. City Hall is on the left.

top right: The yard at Dublin Castle.

left: City Hall. Seán Connolly was shot dead on the roof on Monday afternoon.

Plunkett joined the head of the column wearing his sword. Because of his age, Clarke had traveled ahead in a car accompanied by Mac Diarmada. The two waited for the main column outside the GPO.

As the main body, which had assembled at Liberty Hall, set off for the GPO, a smaller group under Seán Connolly (no relation to James Connolly), an actor with the Abbey Theatre, was dispatched to Dublin Castle. Alongside him was Helena Moloney.

In his office inside the castle, an increasingly worried Nathan continued his discussions with Major Price, the chief intelligence officer. They had been joined by the senior civil servant in charge of the Irish postal and communications services, an Englishman called Sir Arthur Hamilton Norway, who had left his office at the GPO to make his way to Dublin Castle. Ironically, as he made his way to the castle, he would have passed James Connolly and Pearse at the head of the rebels making their way to the GPO. As they began to discuss the security threat, the three men heard a shot in the upper castle yard. Major Price

immediately understood its significance. "They have commenced," he announced to his companions before drawing his revolver and rushing into the yard to fire at the retreating rebels. As the rebels attempted to gain entry to the castle, Sergeant James O'Brien, a 48-year-old, unarmed Dublin Metropolitan policeman from County Limerick, attempted to bar the way. Seán Connolly shot him dead. He was the day's first fatality. He would not be the last.

Following Major Price's arrival, Connolly and his followers inexplicably withdrew. The castle had been at their mercy had they but known it. There was only one armed guard between them and its capture. Although miscalculation on both sides had profound significance in the dynamics of the Rising, the failure to take Dublin Castle was the first in a series of strategic failures that would fatally undermine the rebels' attempts to hold Dublin. They withdrew from the castle gates to the nearby City Hall. Later that day, Seán Connolly was to lose his life when he was shot at his post in City Hall by a sniper firing from the castle.

By now the rebel outposts had been secured. Most of the leaders were in the GPO with the main garrison: MacDonagh, one of only two signatories of the Proclamation not in the GPO, took command of Jacob's Biscuit Factory; the other, Ceannt, was in charge of the Fourth Battalion, which occupied the South Dublin Union. Éamon de Valera was in command of the garrison stationed in Boland's Mill. Edward (Ned) Daly, brother-in-law of Tom Clarke, was commandant of the First Battalion, which had taken possession of the Four Courts. Another group of the Irish Citizen Army under the command of Michael Mallin and Countess Markievicz occupied St Stephen's Green.

Back in the GPO, Connolly, Pearse, and their followers were establishing their headquarters.

I had an Irish tweed costume, with a Sam Browne [belt]. I had my own revolver and ammunition. At the last minute when we were going off at twelve o clock Connolly gave out revolvers to our girls, saying: 'Don't use them except as a last resort.' There were nine girls in our party going to the Castle. We were to attack the castle. It was expected that the psychological effect of attacking Dublin Castle, the citadel of foreign rule for seven hundred years, would be considerable. . . . It was at the Castle the first shot was fired. . . .

I with my girls followed Seán Connolly and his party. We went right up to the Castle Gate, up the narrow street. Just then, a police sergeant came out. . . . When Connolly went to go past him the sergeant put out his arm; and Connolly shot him dead. When the military guard saw that it was serious, he pulled the gates to.

—Helena Moloney, witness statement[12]

I was talking to Sir Matthew Nathan in his office not twenty five yards from the gate when the firing commenced. I said 'they have commenced' and ran to see a policeman lying in a pool of blood and half a dozen Volunteers in green coats dashing about. I fired a few shots from a revolver and then they broke their way into a house on the opposite side. They could have done it as easily as possible [i.e. seized the castle]. Twenty five determined men could have done it. I think there was only a corporal's guard there at the time.

—Major Ivor Price[13]

opposite: Sergeant James O'Brien, the first fatality of the Rising.

above: Illustration of Jacob's Biscuit Factory, ca. 1916, garrisoned by Volunteers under the command of Thomas MacDonagh.

left: St Stephen's Green seen from the Shelbourne Hotel.

Boland's Mill, garrisoned by Volunteers under the command of Éamon de Valera.

Bemused customers were asked to leave and the windows were sandbagged.

That afternoon curious onlookers gathered as Pearse, dressed in his Volunteer uniform, stood under the high portico flanked by his colleagues and read the Proclamation of the Irish Republic. When he finished reading from the Proclamation, James Connolly grasped his hand and said aloud, "Thanks be to God, Pearse, we have lived to see this day."

By late afternoon, the GPO was firmly in rebel hands, their flags flying proudly aloft: one was the green, white, and orange tricolor, which by now had become the symbol of Irish republicanism; the other was a green flag with an Irish harp and the words "The Irish Republic" painted in gold.

Throughout the day, Volunteer reinforcements continued to arrive, including Cumann na mBan and ICA women. Many of the reinforcements

The Four Courts, garrisoned by Volunteers under the command of Edward (Ned) Daly.

POBLACHT NA H EIREANN.

THE PROVISIONAL GOVERNMENT
OF THE
IRISH REPUBLIC
TO THE PEOPLE OF IRELAND.

IRISHMEN AND IRISHWOMEN: In the name of God and of the dead generations from which she receives her old tradition of nationhood, Ireland, through us, summons her children to her flag and strikes for her freedom.

Having organised and trained her manhood through her secret revolutionary organisation, the Irish Republican Brotherhood, and through her open military organisations, the Irish Volunteers and the Irish Citizen Army, having patiently perfected her discipline, having resolutely waited for the right moment to reveal itself, she now seizes that moment, and, supported by her exiled children in America and by gallant allies in Europe, but relying in the first on her own strength, she strikes in full confidence of victory.

We declare the right of the people of Ireland to the ownership of Ireland, and to the unfettered control of Irish destinies, to be sovereign and indefeasible. The long usurpation of that right by a foreign people and government has not extinguished the right, nor can it ever be extinguished except by the destruction of the Irish people. In every generation the Irish people have asserted their right to national freedom and sovereignty; six times during the past three hundred years they have asserted it in arms. Standing on that fundamental right and again asserting it in arms in the face of the world, we hereby proclaim the Irish Republic as a Sovereign Independent State, and we pledge our lives and the lives of our comrades-in-arms to the cause of its freedom, of its welfare, and of its exaltation among the nations.

The Irish Republic is entitled to, and hereby claims, the allegiance of every Irishman and Irishwoman. The Republic guarantees religious and civil liberty, equal rights and equal opportunities to all its citizens, and declares its resolve to pursue the happiness and prosperity of the whole nation and of all its parts, cherishing all the children of the nation equally, and oblivious of the differences carefully fostered by an alien government, which have divided a minority from the majority in the past.

Until our arms have brought the opportune moment for the establishment of a permanent National Government, representative of the whole people of Ireland and elected by the suffrages of all her men and women, the Provisional Government, hereby constituted, will administer the civil and military affairs of the Republic in trust for the people.

We place the cause of the Irish Republic under the protection of the Most High God, Whose blessing we invoke upon our arms, and we pray that no one who serves that cause will dishonour it by cowardice, inhumanity, or rapine. In this supreme hour the Irish nation must, by its valour and discipline and by the readiness of its children to sacrifice themselves for the common good, prove itself worthy of the august destiny to which it is called.

Signed on Behalf of the Provisional Government,

THOMAS J. CLARKE,
SEAN Mac DIARMADA,   THOMAS MacDONAGH,
P. H. PEARSE,   EAMONN CEANNT,
JAMES CONNOLLY.   JOSEPH PLUNKETT.

left: The Proclamation of the Irish Republic as read by Pádraig Pearse outside the GPO, Easter Monday.

above: Painting of Pádraig Pearse as president of the Irish Republic, by Leo Whelan.

The city bore its usual aspect that Monday morning as I went down to my Sackville Street club, where I read the papers, and then went into my office, a few houses away, intending to write letters, and remain till lunch. I was still in the midst of my first letter, when my telephone rang, and Sir Matthew Nathan spoke, asking me to go up to the Castle. He gave no reason, but I surmised some need for such steps as he had suggested two days before. I locked my desk, gave the key of my room to the porter, who was the only person on duty, the day being a bank holiday, and left, saying I should be back in half an hour. I never saw my room again until the whole building was gutted and burnt to a shell.

I saw nothing unusual as I walked up to the Castle. Nathan had with him Major Price, the Army Intelligence Officer. He turned to me as I came in, and told me there was serious trouble in Kerry, where a ship had been seized with German officers on board and material for a rising. Casement, however, whom he then named, had been conveyed to London under guard, with no attempt at rescue. The position was serious, and he desired me to take immediate steps for denying the use of the Telephone and Telegraph service over large areas of Southern Ireland to all but military and Naval use. I said that was too important a matter to be settled verbally, and I must have it in writing. 'Very well,' he said, 'You write out what you want, and I will sign it.' I was just finishing the necessary order, when a volley of musketry crashed out beneath the window. I looked up. 'What's that?' I asked. 'Oh, that's probably the long promised attack on the Castle,' cried Nathan, jumping up and leaving the room, while Major Price shouted from the window to some person below, after which he too ran off. I waited for a few minutes, and then went downstairs in search of some explanation. At the foot of the staircase I found all the messengers huddled together in a frightened crowd. They had just seen the policeman at the gate shot through the heart. They were badly shaken.

They had however got the gate of the Upper Castle yard shut. The gate of the lower yard had also been shut. No attack was proceeding, and I found Nathan with the Store keeper breaking open the armoury in the hope of arming the handful of constables of the Dublin Metropolitan Police who formed the only guard of the Castle. He found some revolvers, but no cartridges; so that the constables remained of little use, while the rebels, declaring themselves without opposition, ranged at will about the city, seizing one important building after another, and posting their proclamation of the Irish Republic wherever they would. In the handsome building of the General Post Office, which I had left so short a while before, the Union Jack was hauled down, and the green flag of the Irish Republic floated in its place. The Office in fact was rushed twenty minutes after I had left it, my room being appropriated for the rebel headquarters. The guard soldiers at the door of the Instrument room did their best, but for some military reason, which I never heard, they had been deprived of ammunition, without my knowledge. Their rifles being empty, they retreated inside and barricaded the door. But the rebels fired through it, shot the sergeant in the face and, the post being untenable, the men surrendered. Had I not been rung up by the Under Secretary, I should have been the only man armed upon the premises. What then should I have done? I presume I ought to have tried to hold the staircase, and keep the mob down.

—Sir Arthur Hamilton Norway, Secretary of the GPO[15]

At 12.10 I was informed that the Sinn Fein Volunteers were taking control of the Public Counter and after a short time I heard the breaking of glass in the lower storey. On looking out a window in the telephone room I saw that the windows of the Public office and other windows looking into Sackville Street were being smashed, the fragments of glass falling on to and covering the pavement, and several members of the Sinn Fein party stood round the public entrance with rifles and revolvers. I at once got Mr. P. Kelly to 'phone to Headquarters of the Army Command, the Police Office in the Castle, and also to Marlboro Barracks asking for assistance. . . .

At 12.30 I was informed by the Sergt. of the Guard that the Rebels were forcing the stairs leading from Henry Street to the Instrument Room and he asked me to obtain assistance. The guard consisted of a Sergeant and 4 men. The passage leading from the head of the stairs to the Instrument Room was then barricaded from the inside by filling it with chairs, wastepaper boxes, etc. in order to delay the entry of the attackers as much as possible, the guard of 1 Sergeant and 4 men standing inside the Instrument Room prepared to receive the rebels if they broke through the obstructions.

—Samuel Guthrie, GPO employee[16]

Commandant Mallin gave me my first dispatch to carry to headquarters at the general post-office. As I crossed O'Connell Street, I had to ride through the great crowds of people who had gathered to hear Padraic Pearse read the proclamation of the republic at the foot of Nelson's Pillar. They had to scatter when the Fifth Lancers—the first of the military forces to learn that the insurgents had taken possession of the post-office—rode in among them to attack the post-office. . . .

When I reached the open space in front of the post-office, I saw two or three men and horses lying in the street, killed by the first volley from the building. It was several days before these horses were taken away, and there was something in the sight of the dumb beasts that hurt me every time I had to pass them. . . .

Even while I was cycling toward the post-office, the crowd had reassembled to watch the raising of the flag of the Irish Republic. As the tricolor—green, white, and orange—appeared above the roof of the post-office, a salute was fired. . . .

Inside the post office our men were busy putting things to right after the lancers' attack. They were getting ready for prolonged resistance. Window-panes were smashed, and barricades set up to protect men who soon would be shooting from behind them. Provisions were brought over from Liberty Hall, where they had long been stored against this day. But what impressed me most was the way the men went at it, as though this was the usual sort of thing to be doing and all in the day's work. There was no sign of excitement, but there was a tenseness, a sense of expectancy, a kind of exaltation, that was almost more than I could bear.

—Margaret Skinnider[17]

had just learned of the Rising and wished to participate. Among them was The O'Rahilly, who had just arrived back from his attempts to enforce Mac-Neill's countermanding order. "I helped to wind the clock," he is reported to have said, "I might as well hear it strike."

Despite their success in seizing and holding their main targets on Easter Monday, the rebels made some fundamental errors, including the failure to take Dublin Castle and the Shelbourne Hotel, which overlooked their position in St Stephen's Green. The rebels also made no attempt to occupy Trinity College Dublin, which occupied a highly strategic position in the center of the city. They assumed that it would be heavily guarded by

top: South Dublin Union, garrisoned by Volunteers under the command of Éamonn Ceannt.

bottom: Trinity College from Dame Street.

One of my men on the windows on Monday afternoon told me that I was required at the window, that there were two strange looking men outside and I went to the window and saw two obviously foreign men. Judging by the appearance of their faces I took them to be seamen. I asked what they wanted. The smaller of the two spoke. He said: 'I am from Sweden, my friend from Finland. We want to fight. May we come in?' I asked him why a Swede and a Finn would want to fight against the British. . . . He had come in on a ship, and they were part of a crew. . . . So I said: 'Tell me why do you want to come in and fight against England.' He said: 'Finland, a small country, Russia eat her up'. Then he said: 'Sweden, another small country, Russia eat her up too. Russia with the British, therefore we against'. I said, 'Can you fight. Do you know how to use a weapon?' He said: 'I can use a rifle. My friend no. He can use what you shoot the fowl with'. I said: 'A shotgun'. I decided to admit them. I took them in and got the Swede a rifle, the Finn a shotgun.

—Liam Tannam, captain, GPO garrison, witness statement [19]

Easter Monday, a holiday, was warm and many people went to the races, to the Hill of Howth, Killiney, or to the mountains. I walked across the city over the Liffey. . . . I looked at the statue of Justice on the upper Castle Gate. She had her back to the city, and I remembered that it had frequently been commented on, satirically. I passed by Trinity College; the heavy oaken doors were closed. In O'Connell Street large groups of people were gathered together. From the flagstaff on top of the General Post Office, the GPO, floated a new flag, a tri-coloured one of green, white and orange, the colours running out from the mast.

"What's it all about?" I asked a man who stood near me with a scowl on his face.

"Those boyhoes, the Volunteers, have seized the Post Office. They want nothing less than a republic," he laughed scornfully. . . .

The windows had been smashed. Heavy mail bags half-filled the space, rifle barrels projected, officers in uniform with yellow tabs could be seen hurrying through the rooms. Outside, men were carrying in heavy bundles—"explosives, I bet, or ammunition," said a man beside me.

Others unloaded provisions and vegetables and carried the food inside. On the flat roof sentries patrolled to and fro. . . .

Behind Nelson's Pillar lay dead horses, some with their feet in the air, other lying flat. . . . Seated on a dead horse was a woman, a shawl around her head, untidy wisps of hair straggled across her dirty face. She swayed slowly, drunk, singing:

Boys in Khaki, Boys in Blue, Here's the best of Jolly Good Luck to You.

On the base of the Pillar was a white poster. Gathered around were groups of men and women. Some looked at it with serious faces, others laughed and sniggered. I began to read it with a smile but my smile ceased as I read.

Poblacht na hEireann The Provisional Government of the IRISH REPUBLIC *To The People of Ireland*

—Ernie O'Malley, Dublin student, later republican activist [20]

We were standing in the main street (Sackville St) about 2pm just about one hundred yards from our hotel. Shots were being fired and a soldier from the Dublin Fusiliers was killed while walking with his young lady. There were thousands of people in the streets and all of a sudden a large motor-car whizzed past us. In it was the noted Countess dressed in a green uniform. As she went past she fired two shots at us. One went over our heads, the other caught an elderly man in the arm. It seemed to be like a signal to the other Sinn Féiners for bullets started to whizz all around us. As we were unarmed and had our Red Cross badges on us we went for our lives to the Soldiers' Club. The proprietor told us that all the soldiers had gone over to Trinity College which is the headquarters of the Dublin University Officers' Training Corps.

—Corporal John Garland, one of the New Zealand soldiers caught up in the Rising, in a letter to his father in Auckland [21]

the university's Officer Training Corps. It was not, as they were enjoying the Easter holiday. Trinity College was used to great effect later in the week to target rebel positions. But most of the rebels' problems were due to having fewer men than they had expected.

The British response was slow initially, with only four hundred regular troops on duty in barracks in Dublin when the Rising started. As news of the events trickled out, the authorities struggled to regain control. The first major engagement occurred at the GPO when a party of Lancers charged up the street with sabers drawn and were fired on by rebels. Three troopers were killed, together with a number of their horses.

As the day wore on, sporadic fighting occurred throughout the city. Some of the fiercest took place at the South Dublin Union as the men

British Lancers pass a dead horse in Dublin city center.

At about 4.00 pm. N. returned from a tour of inspection, and told me all was quiet in Sackville Street, and begged me to go out with him and see the G.P.O.

I quaked rather, but we set off and reached Sackville Street safely.

Over the fine building of the G.P.O. floated a great green flag with the words "Irish Republic" on it in large white letters. Every window on the ground floor was smashed and barricaded with furniture, and a big placard announced "The Headquarters of the Provisional Government of the Irish Republic." At every window were two men with rifles, and on the roof the parapet was lined with men. . . .

We stood opposite and were gazing, when suddenly two shots were fired, and, seeing there was likely to be an ugly rush, I fled again, exhorting N. to take refuge at the club.

He never reached the club, but came back to the hotel and we had tea, and then we went to inspect St. Stephen's Green.

He found all round the Green, just inside the railings among the shrubberies, the rebels had dug deep pits or holes, and in every hole were three men. They had barricaded the Street opposite the Shelbourne Hotel, and there had been a lot of firing and several people killed, and shots had gone into the hotel, which is, as you know, a fine building facing the Green.

—Lady Norway [22]

When I reported with the car to Commandant Mallin in Stephen's Green, he told me that he must keep me. He said that owing to MacNeill's calling off the Volunteers a lot of the men who should have been under him had had to be distributed around other posts, and that few of those left him were trained to shoot, so I must stay and be ready to take up the work of a sniper. He took me round the Green and showed me how the barricading of the gates and digging trenches had begun, and he left me in charge of this work while he went to superintend the erection of barricades in the streets and arrange other work. About two hours later he definitely promoted me to be his second in command. The work was very exciting when the fighting began. I continued round and round the Green, reporting back if anything was wanted, or tackling any sniper who was particularly objectionable.

—Countess Markievicz [23]

At six o'clock that evening, just when it was beginning to grow dusk, on my way back from the post-office I noticed that the crowd of curious civilians who had been hanging about the Green all day had quite disappeared. The next thing I saw was two persons hurrying away from the Green. These were Town Councilor Partridge and the countess. They came to a halt in the street just ahead of me. Then I saw the British soldiers coming up Harcourt Street!

The countess stood motionless, waiting for them to come near. She was a lieutenant in the Irish Volunteers and, in her officer's uniform and black hat with great plumes, looked most impressive. At length she raised her gun to her shoulder—it was an "automatic" over a foot long, which she had converted into a short rifle by taking out the wooden holster and using it as a stock—and took aim. Neither she nor Partridge noticed me as I came up behind them. I was quite close when they fired. The shots rang out at the same moment, and I saw the two officers leading the column drop to the street. As the countess was taking aim again, the soldiers, without firing a shot, turned and ran in great confusion for their barracks. The whole company fled as fast as they could from *two* people, one of them a woman! When you consider, however, that for years these

soldiers had been going about Dublin as if they owned it; that now they did not know from what house or street corner they might be fired upon by men in green uniforms, it is not to be wondered that they were temporarily demoralized.

—Margaret Skinnider [24]

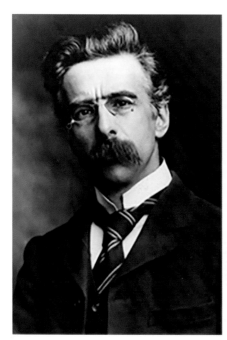

John Joly.

Easter Monday, April 24th, 1916 . . . I was in Trinity College by four o'clock. I had already been in the city that same morning visiting a friend. There were then no signs of the fatal events proceeding elsewhere. The Post Office was actually being seized at the time I was sitting with my sick friend. But now how different! Carriage traffic had almost ceased and crowds hurried, partly in terror, partly in curiosity, about the streets. An occasional shot was heard. But it soon became evident that the Rebels were virtually in possession of the city.

I left Trinity cautiously by one of the side gates. I was anxious to ascertain, if possible, the magnitude of the movement and to get some idea of the numbers engaged in it. I visited the General Post Office, the central building in Sackville Street. It was a wreck. Glass littered deeply the path and pavement in front of it. Armed men stood behind its shattered windows. Useless barricades had been piled up within—mail bags, evidently filled with letters, to keep out bullets! Chairs and tables through which bullets would pass almost as easily! And, peering out from their defences, the unhappy warriors threatened with their rifles the scared crowd, which alternatively

approached and ran away. At one window a mere boy was still knocking out the glass with the butt of his rifle. Above the building floated a huge green banner with the inscription in white letters, "Irish Republic". Truly Der Tag had come! But oh, how pitiful! A fantastic chimera, and death the sure and certain wage!

The Rebels were moving about freely in the streets. All seemed armed with rifles. The police had entirely disappeared. They had done all they could, and some had offered their lives in a vain endeavour to save the city. St. Stephen's Green, which I next visited, was closed. A sort of barrier had been placed with the large gate facing the foot of Grafton Street. Behind it stood, with set face and in Sinn Fein uniform, an armed man. He held his rifle at the ready. But neither military nor police contested his supremacy. . . . A man in the small crowd remarked to me on the juvenile appearance of these Sinn Feiners. What, indeed, could they know of right and wrong? What could they do to save themselves even if they knew the truth? It was a pitiful sight. . . .

I returned to the College but little wiser than when I had left it. . . . Trinity College seemed almost without

defenders. Major Tate, the C.O., was unfortunately away. But Captain Alton of the O.T.C., Lieutenant Luce of the Royal Irish Rifles, who was home from the front on sick leave, and Lieutenant Waterhouse were fortunately at hand. A few boys in khaki were about. There was no doubt of the seriousness of the position. Help from military or police was not to be expected for some time—possibly for some days. That the College had not already been captured was most inexplicable. It was obviously the most central and commanding position in the city. There was the additional attraction of the military stores of the O.T.C. depot. In this were kept some hundreds of service rifles and many thousands of rounds of ammunition. The loot of the buildings would supply many requirements of those in possession. And once captured nothing but the wholesale destruction of buildings, containing the most precious heirlooms of the ancient University, would suffice to dislodge the enemy.

—John Joly, Chair of Geology and Minerology, Trinity College, writing as "anonymous member of the Trinity garrison" in *Blackwood's Magazine*, July 1916[25]

We reported there [Trinity College] at 3pm. There were only about thirty of us and we filled sandbags from 5pm until 9pm. By that time our strength had grown to nearly sixty including five New Zealanders, one Australian, five from South Africa and two Canadian. At 11pm they woke us up and took the colonials whom they called Anzacs (although there were really only six Anzacs) to the roof where we were to snipe.... From the roof we could command a view of the main streets—Sackville, Grafton, Dame. Four of us were on the front parapet commanding Dame St and a part of Grafton St.

—Corporal John Garland [26]

I went back again to the City Hall. Soon after that, at two o'clock, Sean Connolly, who was on the roof, was hit by a stray bullet and killed. Dr. Lynn was still there. She came up and attended him. She said: "I'm afraid he is gone." He was bleeding very much from the stomach. I said the act of contrition into his ear. We had no priest. We were very distressed at Sean Connolly's death, I particularly, as I had known him for so long and acted with him. His young brother Matt, who was only fifteen, was also on the roof and cried bitterly when he saw his brother dying.

—Helena Moloney, witness statement [27]

Insurrection broke out at noon today in Dublin when attack made on Castle but not pressed home. Since then large hostile parties have occupied Stephen's Green and various parties have held up troops marching from barracks firing on them and on houses. City hall, Post Office, Westland row station occupied by Sinn Feiners. Some railway bridges blown up and telegraphic communication generally interrupted. Have information of two policemen, one officer and half a dozen soldiers killed but casualties may be much more numerous. Situation at present not satisfactory but understand troops now beginning to arrive from Curragh.

—Telegraph from Nathan to Birrell, Easter Monday evening

Towards evening, we saw a large company—probably a hundred men—going into the Castle. I believe they got troops in quickly through Ship Street too. There was now a large garrison in the Castle. At about half past eight or nine o'clock, when nightfall came, there was a sudden bombardment. It came suddenly on us. On the roof level, on which there were glass windows, and through the windows on the ground floor of the City hall, there were machine bullets pouring in.... At this time, the firing was very intense. A window was smashed in at the back and then we knew they were pouring in and they did come in at the back. A voice said "Surrender, in the name of the King". At this point, I felt a pluck on my arm and our youngest girl, Annie Norgrove—there are three or four sisters of them—said to me, "Miss Moloney, Miss Moloney, we are not going to give in? Mr Connolly said we were not to surrender." She was terrified but there was no surrender about her. The call for surrender was repeated. "How many are here? Surrender." I heard Dr. Lynn quite close over near the window. She apparently was near them in the round circular hall. "Surrender", they called out again. Then we were taken.

—Helena Moloney, witness statement [28]

Kingsbridge Station.

under Éamonn Ceannt's command fought off a counterattack. As evening approached, British reinforcements had arrived from the Curragh and were preparing to dislodge the rebels from some of their outposts, including City Hall, to which Sean Connolly and his small Citizen Army group had withdrawn. Connolly himself had been shot earlier on the roof as he inspected army positions in the castle. The larger ICA group, under Michael Mallin, had barricaded St Stephen's Green and inexplicably dug trenches, leaving the Shelbourne Hotel, which overlooked their positions, untouched. Mallin had by now been joined by Countess Markievicz. She had set out to tour the rebel positions but had been asked by Mallin to stay on as his second-in-command. There were a number of civilian casualties: one man was shot as he remonstrated with rebels who had taken his cart to build a barricade.

With rumors sweeping the city and the sound of gunfire still continuing, few in Dublin that night slept soundly. British troops continued to arrive at Kingsbridge Station throughout the night. Also to arrive from the Curragh was Brigadier General W. H. M. Lowe and the 25th Infantry Reserve Brigade. He immediately took command of British forces in Dublin. Lowe's plan was to throw a cordon around the city, cutting off the GPO and the Four Courts from the outlying garrisons, and then tighten the noose.

Brigadier General Lowe.

After dinner N. went out to see if he could get near the Castle, but he found awful fighting. The troops were storming the City Hall and using machine-guns, and it was too unhealthy for him to get near, so he came back at 9 and went to bed.

I stayed up in case of being wanted on the 'phone, and at 11.30 p.m. went up to my room, and a few minutes later H. walked in, to my immense relief.

The troops had arrived from the Curragh at about 5 p.m. and had promptly stormed the City Hall, which commanded the main gate of the Castle, and had taken it after fierce fighting.

H. saw prisoners being brought into the Castle yard, and when all was quiet he and several other officials crept out and reached their various homes.

People are appalled at the utter unpreparedness of the Government. In the face of a huge body of trained and armed men, openly revolutionary, they had taken no precautions whatever for the defence of the city in the event of an outbreak.

—Lady Norway[29]

Tuesday, April 25

By daybreak, it became apparent that the arrival of British reinforcements had made an immediate impact on rebel positions. At St Stephen's Green, soldiers managed to place a machine gun on the roof of the Shelbourne Hotel and opened up on the rebel positions below, to devastating effect. Mallin, Markievicz, and those under their command had little choice under the withering fire but to withdraw across the green to the nearby College of Surgeons.

Machine guns were also deployed on the roof of Trinity College, and four eighteen-pounder field guns as well as additional troops were brought from Athlone into Trinity. By early morning, rebel positions were under heavy fire. Despite the intensification of the British response, morale was high in the GPO, which had not yet seen a direct attack. The rebels were still hopeful of a country-wide rising, a hope that, apart from a number of isolated incidents at Ashbourne, County Meath, Enniscorthy, County Wexford, and parts of East Galway, would prove illusory. The rebels in the GPO, however, had another problem on their hands. By late on Monday, the authorities had withdrawn all of the Dublin Metropolitan Police from the streets. Ordinary civic life had broken down. There was great anger among the "separation women," who were in receipt of an allowance from the authorities for their husbands and fathers who were fighting with the British Army in Europe. With the postal system shut down, they were unable to collect their money to feed their families and were quick to show their hostility to the rebels. The area surrounding Sackville Street was one of the poorest in Europe, and many of the people who lived in the tenements took advantage of the breakdown in law and order. Crowds poured into the streets, looting and destroying shops. The rebels were horrified. Appeals by Sean Mac Diarmada and other rebel leaders fell on deaf ears. One well-known Dublin figure, pacifist and socialist Francis Sheehy Skeffington, was on the streets appealing for calm and doing his best to stop the looting. His journey, however, would turn out to be a deadly one.

Further reinforcements arrived throughout the day. By evening some 6,627 British troops were in Dublin. That night martial law was declared in Ireland for the first time in a century.

All night the firing continued. Between 1 and 2 a.m. it was awful, and I lay and quaked. It was all in the direction of the Castle.

This morning we hear the military are pouring into the city, and are in the Shelbourne Hotel and Trinity College.

The rebels have barricaded Sackville Street, and it is expected to be very fierce fighting over the G.P.O. It is terrible!

—Lady Norway[30]

The sun rose at 4 a.m. on a beautiful summer-like day with a slight breeze coming through the GPO's many glassless windows. O'Connell Street was eerily silent, empty of people and with its cobbles snow-white with sheets of paper. Not a living thing is in sight. Even the birds shun the district.

—Dick Humphries, GPO garrison[31]

opposite: Dependents of Irish soldiers in British Army, waiting for allowances.

Got up before the rest of the household and walked down to Earlsfort Terrace to the corner of Stephen's Green to see if it had been evacuated during the night as I felt perfectly certain it must have been, for it appeared to me to be a place impossible to defend for any length of time, as all the trenches and cover for snipers could be reached by machine guns and rifle fire from the tops of the surrounding houses. To my astonishment I found that not only had it not been evacuated but that a lively interchange of shots was going on from all sides, but who was firing and from where I could not see. Walked back up Earlsfort Terrace. Met Miss Boland and Miss Barton coming back from mass and stood talking with them in the middle of the street when a machine gun went off with so loud a noise that I was sure it was fired from the scaffolding of University Building 40 or 50 yards behind me and three bullets lodged in the window and rain pipe of a disused house in Earlsfort Terrace about 8 feet over my head. I felt inclined to jump but was ashamed and walked in as leisurely a manner as I could up the rest of the Terrace, but did not feel in any way comfortable. Though I thought at the time that the shots came from just behind me, I think now that they were fired from a machine gun stationed on the top of Dr. Gogarty's house next the Shelbourne Hotel which had been occupied by the military. If so it was criminally careless of them to shoot up a street in which there were only two or three women and myself walking quietly and from which no shots had at any time been fired.

—Douglas Hyde, diary,
Tuesday, April 25 [32]

There can be no doubt that the accurate fire maintained from the College was an important factor in the salvation of the city....The whole length of Westmoreland Street was kept clear by the College rifles; and even the strongholds of the enemy in Sackville Street were assailed from the northern edge of the College. Regarding the position as a whole, the grounds and building of Trinity College filled the function of a loyal nucleus, dividing the forces of the rebels and keeping open to the troops some of the principal thoroughfares of the City.

—John Joly,
Trinity College garrison [33]

It seems the British had taken possession of a hotel at one side of the Green—the Hotel Shelbourne—and had placed a machine-gun on the roof. At four o'clock in the morning they began firing.

The chill I was having woke me, but I quickly followed the others to their hiding-place. From the first we were aware that had we taken possession of all buildings around the Green, according to our original plan, this morning salute of the British would have been impossible. As it was, our intrenchments and barricades proved of no avail. We realized at once we should have to evacuate the Green and retire into the College of Surgeons....

One of our boys was killed before we got inside the College of Surgeons. Had the British gunners been better trained for their task, we might have lost more, for we were completely at their mercy from the moment they began to fire at dawn until the big door of the college closed, and we took up the defense of our new position in the great stone fortress.

Every time I left the college, I was forced to run the gauntlet of this machine-gun. I blessed the enemy's bad marksmanship several times a day. To be sure, they tried hard enough to hit something.

—Margaret Skinnider [34]

We got our first bag on Tuesday morning at 4am when three Sinn Féiners came along on bikes evidently going from Shepherds' Green [sic] to the GPO. The men on my left, as soon as they saw them coming, told us to mark the last man and they would get the first two. We all fired at once . . . the chap we killed, he had four bullet marks on him which meant that we all got him and that he must have been killed instantly. A peculiar thing had happened. After he was killed he still sat on his bike and continued on for about thirty yards on the free-wheel. I though we had missed him when all of a sudden the bike swerved and he came off. This chap was a platoon leader and on him they found a list of the names and addresses of his platoon, and two dispatches, together with some money that he had evidently taken from the GPO.

—Corporal John Garland,
describing the shooting of
Volunteer Gerald Keogh
outside Trinity College [35]

The Anzacs [Australian and New Zealand Army Corps] had been above on the roof of the College since an early hour. Owing to the strict order received from the Irish Command not to fire until attacked, many chances of "potting" Rebels had been missed. But later in the morning this order had been withdrawn. Already before daylight a dispatch-rider of the enemy had been brought down by the fire of the Anzacs. It was wonderful shooting. He was one of the three who were riding past on bicycles. Four shots were fired. Three found their mark in the head of the unfortunate victim. Another of the riders was wounded and escaped on foot. The third abandoned his bicycle and also escaped. This shooting was done by the uncertain light of the electric lamps, and at a high angle downwards from a lofty building. The body was brought in.

Later I saw him. In no irreverent spirit I lifted the face-cloth. He looked quite young: one might almost call him a boy. The handsome waxen face was on one side concealed in blood. Poor boy! What crime was his? That of listening to the insane wickedness and folly preached by those older and who ought to be wiser than he. And was not he, after all, but one of those who carry to its logical conclusion the long crusade against English rule which for generations has kept peace from Irish hearts? More honest than many of his teachers, he has been led into crime and now pays the penalty. It is true, if truth exists at all, that this life cut short and the rancour and bitterness with which it was filled are as much the handiwork of the constitutional agitator as of many who are doomed to summary execution for this night's work. When will England appreciate the Irish temperament? When will our rulers learn that these rash and foolish sons of the Empire require quiet and resolute government, sane education, and protection from the fanatic and the agitator, to whose poison they are at present exposed from their earliest years?

—John Joly,
Trinity College garrison [36]

It was Sackville Street with the accent on the 'sack'! The street was crowded, and the worst of the slum population—the wretched folk who inhabit the tenements formed of the old mansions of the dead and gone, or emigrated aristocracy—were about in great and quite universal force. A filthy guttersnipe with an old fowling piece was menacing an aged man, and a few steps further a dirty unwashed woman of the slums, ragged and unkempt, with her matted hair surmounted by a fashionable hat, shuffled past, her dirty naked feet thrust into fashionable patent-leather shoes. The pavement was ankle deep in finely broken plate glass, shattered by blows in order to place the shopkeeper's stock at the mercy of the itching fingers from the slums. The thieves and bad characters of Dublin had swarmed from their dens into Sackville Street. What a scene. Had I been a photographic plate, exposed in Sackville Street that Easter Tuesday morning, I could have presented one phase of the French Revolution in miniature.

—Henry Crawford Hartnell,
writer and journalist [37]

The mob were chiefly women and children with a sprinkling of men. They swarmed in and out of the side door bearing huge consignments of banana, the great bunches on the stalk, to which the children attached a cord and ran away dragging it along. . . . It was an amazing sight, and nothing daunted these people. Higher up at another shop we were told a woman was hanging out of a window and dropping down loot to a friend, when she was shot through the head by a sniper . . . the body dropped into the street and the mob cleared. In a few minutes a hand-cart appeared and gathered up the body, and instantly all the mob swarmed back to continue the joyful proceedings!

—Lady Norway [38]

Wednesday, April 26

In the early hours of Wednesday morning the first troopships sent from England arrived at Kingstown Harbor. The troops were members of the Sherwood Foresters, raw recruits, many of whom had never fired their rifles. Some indeed thought they had landed in France.

The troops made their way to the various British barracks in the city. Two battalions reached Kilmainham and Kingsbridge without incident. The other two battalions took the coastal route to Beggars Bush Barracks and Trinity College. Their journey would be very different. The rebel garrison at Boland's Mill had posted a number of men at two outposts to guard against reinforcements crossing Mount Street Bridge. Two men, Mick Malone and Jimmy Grace, took over a room in 25 Northumberland Road. Another small outpost of seven Volunteers was positioned in Clanwilliam House, which had a commanding view of the bridge across which the troops would have to cross if they managed to escape the firing from Northumberland Road. As the column of troops approached, the first volleys rang out from no. 25. The shooting from

Front page of the London *Daily Express* on Wednesday, April 26.

left: Members of the Sherwood Foresters on Northumberland Road.

above: Michael Malone.

Mount Street Bridge and Clanwilliam House after the final assault.

Malone and Grace was deadly accurate. Ten soldiers were killed in the first volleys. The inexperienced soldiers found it hard to identify the location of the fire. They regrouped time and again. Time and again they were cut down as the volleys continued to ring out. The battle raged throughout the day and into the evening. It took until 5:00 pm to clear out 25 Northumberland Road. A full frontal assault on the building resulted in the death of Malone; Grace escaped out the back. Night had fallen before sheer strength of numbers eventually turned Clanwilliam House into a blazing inferno. When the action finally ended, the Irish Volunteers had lost eight of their twelve men and the British had 230 dead or wounded. This was one of the few military successes the Volunteers managed during the rebellion.

In other parts of the city, however, the rebels were coming under increasing pressure. Early that morning the first artillery shells from the eighteen-pounder guns that the British had moved into the city fell on Liberty Hall. The gunboat *Helga*, moored on the River Liffey, joined in the bombardment. Liberty Hall was soon a smoking ruin.

James Connolly had long believed that the British would not use artillery in an urban area because, he thought, they would not willingly destroy property. He was proved very wrong. Later that day artillery began to shell various positions in Sackville Street, including the GPO. Lower Sackville Street was systematically being reduced to rubble.

There were first three charges at intervals taken to regroup, and as the British came into sight between the hoarding and the schools they were engaged by us at about 12.30 p.m. The enemy suffered such heavy casualties in the early charges that none of them reached the bridge and those who were not wounded or killed sought cover behind the doorsteps and hedges. Things were very quiet for about an hour and a half except for spasmodic shooting when the British made a determined onslaught on the bridge. Nobody succeeded in crossing the bridge although some went down Percy Place and others turned right along the canal bank. Some of those who went down Percy Place succeeded in getting into some of the houses and some were shot. Those who turned to the right came under our fire from Roberts yard and they were wiped out before they were able to take cover. After an interval of about half an hour or twenty minutes a second and more determined attack was launched on the bridge. Some succeeded in barely crossing the bridge when they were wiped out. . . . Later on a still more determined onslaught than the previous one was made to gain the bridge. This time the enemy succeeded in crossing the bridge and having done so they did not seem to know what their objective was or where they were going. Some turned left towards Warrington Place and others turned right coming down towards Clanwilliam Place. Those who came in our direction were completely wiped out. The bridge and Northumberland Road was strewn with dead and wounded.

—Seamus Kavanagh, member of Clanwilliam House outpost, witness statement[40]

The British gunboat *Helga*.

Liberty Hall following the shelling by the *Helga*.

Wednesday also witnessed one of the most notorious events of the week. The previous evening British soldiers under the command of Captain J. C. Bowen-Colthurst had arrested Francis Sheehy Skeffington, along with two other civilians, when Sheehy Skeffington was making his way home from the city after unsuccessful attempts to stop the looting. At 9:00 am Bowen-Colthurst had his three prisoners taken to the yard in Portobello Barracks and shot. Bowen-Colthurst's actions were reported by a fellow officer, and he was later court-martialed and found insane.

left: Francis Sheehy Skeffington.

right: Captain J. C. Bowen-Colthurst.

Madam had had a fine uniform of green moleskin made for me. With her usual generosity, she had mine made of better material than her own. It consisted of kneebreeches, belted coat, and puttees. I slipped into this uniform, climbed up astride the rafters, and was assigned a loophole through which to shoot. It was dark there, full of smoke and the din of firing, but it was good to be in action. I could look across the tops of trees and see the British soldiers on the roof of the Shelbourne. I could also hear their shot hailing against the roof and wall of our fortress, for in truth this building was just that. More than once I saw the man I aimed at fall. . . .

On Wednesday we spent most of our time sniping at the British from the roof of the College of Surgeons, and on Wednesday night Commandant Mallin sent two squads to cut off some British who had planted a machine gun on the roof of University church. I was in charge of one squad of four men. . . .

It took only a few moments to reach the building we were to set afire. Councilor [William] Partridge smashed the glass door in the front of a shop that occupied the ground floor. He did it with the butt of his rifle and a flash followed. It had been discharged! I rushed past him into the doorway of the shop, calling to the others to come on. Behind me came the sound of a volley, and I fell. It was as I had on the instant divined. The flash had revealed us to the enemy.

"It's all over," I muttered, as I felt myself falling. But a moment later, when I knew I was not dead, I was sure I should pull through. . . .

They laid me on a table and cut away the coat of my fine, new uniform. I cried over that. Then they found I had been shot in three places, my right side under the arm, my right arm, and in the back of my right side. . . .

They had to probe several times to get the bullets, and all the while Madam [Countess Markievicz] held my hand. But the probing did not hurt as much as she expected it would. My disappointment at not being able to bomb the Shelbourne Hotel was what made me unhappy.

—Margaret Skinnider[41]

In spite of that optimism, we all seemed to take it for granted we would finally be crushed. By common consent it was to be a fight to a finish. It was thought that the enemy would rush our position with superior forces and would take it with enormous losses. None of us expected mercy but we felt we would sell our lives dearly. There was no feeling of despondency. The atmosphere was one of subdued excitement and determination—desperation maybe—for we appreciated only too well the odds against us. We talked confidently of holding out for two or three weeks, of being able to make enough noise to draw the attention of the world to this small nation. We would hold our post until the last man's rifle was silenced.

—Jim Ryan,
GPO garrison
medical officer [42]

Early on Wednesday Liberty Hall received its quietus. Two eighteen-pounders and the guns of H.M.S. Helga, brought up the Liffey, were used to demolish it. The noise was tremendous. To the general din was added the spitting of a machine-gun placed high on the tower of the Fire Brigade Station. When next I saw Liberty Hall its empty shell alone remained. Every floor had been blown out of it. It was stated that none of the rebels had remained to face the attack. A few weeks ago I saw armed men keeping guard within this building to keep out the police: and this was known to, and suffered by, the authorities. It was known to, and noted in the press. But nothing was done.

—John Joly,
Trinity College garrison [43]

At night the din increased: artillery was being used. I slipped out of bed, got quietly over the back wall and went downtown. There were few people out. 'It's dangerous to go near O'Connell Street,' a man said 'three people have been badly wounded near the Parnell monument.' I reached the monument and turned into Moore Street. From the GPO came the sound of cheering, then a voice singing:

Then here's their memory—
    let it be
For us a guiding light,
to cheer our strife for liberty and
    teach us to unite!
Though good and ill be Ireland's still,
Though sad as those your fate;
For true men, like you, men
Like those of ninety eight.

Men took up the chorus; their voices echoed through the bullet noise. The unlit streets gave a strange quality to the words, the chorus zoomed in a loud shadow [sic] between rifle crashes. I felt I would like to join in that song. . . . I went back to my home in the early morning and got into bed. . . . I felt faint stirrings of sympathy as I wrote in my diary. I did not feel indifferent now to the men holding Dublin

—Ernie O'Malley,
Dublin student [44]

Royal Commission, Arrest and Treatment of Francis Sheehy Skeffington

We now proceed to describe in order of time the events into which we have been directed to enquire....

8. Mr. Sheehy Skeffington was the first of the three individuals to be arrested: his arrest had no connection with the arrest of Mr. Dickson and Mr. McIntyre, which occurred some three hours later.

9. Mr. Francis Sheehy Skeffington was a well-known figure in Dublin and shortly before 8pm on April 25th he was walking from the city in the direction of his home which was situated at 11 Grosvenor Place, Rathmines. His way led over Portobello Bridge, and about 350 yards further on he would have passed the turning which leads to the main entrance of Portobello Barracks.

10. It was conceded on all hands before us that Mr. Sheehy Skeffington had no connection with the Rebellion; his views were opposed to the use of physical force; and it appears that he has been engaged that afternoon in making some public appeal to prevent looting and the like. Mrs. Sheehy Skeffington gave evidence of this fact, and her evidence is confirmed by a document which was found on him when he was searched and which contained a form of a membership of a proposed civic organisation to check looting. As he approached Portobello Bridge he was followed by a crowd, some of the members of which were shouting out his name....

11. Lieutenant Morris heard people in the street shouting out Mr. Sheehy Skeffington's name, and he determined to detain him and send him to the barracks....

12. We consider that there is no good ground of complaint against the action of Lieutenant Morris in causing Mr. Sheehy Skeffington to be detained and sent to barracks. He told us that he had taken the same course with one or two others who seemed likely to cause a crowd to congregate; his picket had been fired at from time to time....

    No charge was made against Mr. Sheehy Skeffington and he went quite willingly....

13. On arrival at the barracks Mr. Sheehy Skeffington was taken to the main guard room; three young officers named Dobbin, Tooley and Alexander Wilson, were sharing duty there, Mr. Dobbin being the senior of the three....

Evidence as to this interrogation is not quite precise or consistent but the witness agreed that Mr. Sheehy Skeffington stated that he was not a Sinn Feiner, but that he was in favour of passive resistance and opposed to militarism....

14. Mr. Sheehy Skeffington was searched by Captain Bowen-Colthurst. This gentleman was an officer of 16 years' service. He belonged to the Royal Irish Rifles, and had considerable experience of warfare....

    At the time of the Dublin disturbances he was attached to the 3rd Battalion in Portobello Barracks. Having searched Mr. Sheehy Skeffington, Captain Bowen-Colthurst about 9 o'clock handed over to the Adjutant what he had found upon him. The Adjutant made copies of these documents and produced them before us; they were few referred to, which was a draft form of membership for a civic guard. There was nothing of an incriminatory nature found on Mr. Sheehy Skeffington. When we come to deal with the cases of Mr. Dickson and Mr. McIntyre, it will again be seen that nothing of consequence was found upon them, and the absence of compromising documents in all three cases is, in the light of a report subsequently made by Captain Bowen-Colthurst, a fact of considerable importance.

15. Later, on the same evening Captain Bowen-Colthurst went out to the barracks in command of a party under orders to enter and occupy the premises at the corner of Camden Street and Harrington Street occupied by Mr. James Kelly for the purposes of his tobacco business....

16. Captain Bowen-Colthurst adopted the extraordinary and indeed almost meaningless course of taking Mr. Sheehy Skeffington with him as a "hostage". He had no right to take Mr. Sheehy Skeffington out of the custody of the guard for this or any other purpose and he asked no one's leave to do so....

    Before they left the Barracks Mr. Sheehy Skeffington's hands were tied behind his back and Captain Bowen-Colthurst called upon him to say his prayers. Upon Mr. Sheehy Skeffington refusing to do so Captain Bowen-Colthurst ordered the men of his party to take their hats off and himself uttered a prayer, the words of it, according to Lieutenant Wilson's evidence being: "O Lord God, if it shall please thee to take away the life of this man forgive him for Christ's sake." . . .

27. Shortly after 10am, Captain Bowen-Colthurst came to a guard room. He appears on his first arrival to have entirely ignored Lieutenant Dobbin, who was standing in the barrack square near to the guard room entrance, and having passed into the guard room itself to have given his orders direct to the sergeant. These orders were to the effect that he required the three prisoners, Skeffington, Dickson and McIntyre in the yard for the purpose of speaking to them. The yard in question is within the guard room. It comprises a space less than 40ft. in length and some 15ft. in width and is surrounded by high brick walls. . . .

29. During the few moments that were occupied by the calling out of the three prisoners Captain Bowen-Colthurst stepped out of the guard room to the spot where Lieutenant Dobbin was still standing and informed that officer that he was taking the three prisoners out for the purpose of shooting them, as

he thought "it was the best thing to do." Lieutenant Dobbin's recollection is not clear as to whether the three men were mentioned by name, but there is no doubt that their number and the purpose for which Captain Bowen-Colthurst was taking them out were distinctly conveyed to his mind. . . .

32. When Captain Bowen-Colthurst returned into the guard room after his brief statement to Lieutenant Dobbin he ordered some of the guard with their rifles out into the yard where the three prisoners had preceded them. All the men on duty had their magazines already filled, and seven of the guard, who appear to have been merely those that happened at the moment to be nearest the yard passage, accompanied by Sergeant Aldridge followed Captain Bowen-Colthurst out into the yard. What then occurred took place so rapidly that we have little doubt that none of the three victims realised they were about to meet their death. We are confirmed in this view by the fact that all the witnesses, including civilian prisoners in the detention room, to whom everything that took place in the yard was

audible, agree in stating that no sound was uttered by any of the three.

33. While the soldiers were entering the yard Captain Bowen-Colthurst ordered the three prisoners to walk to the wall at the other end, a distance as we have stated of only a few yards. As they were doing this the seven soldiers entering the yard, fell into line along the wall adjoining the entrance and immediately received from Captain Bowen-Colthurst the order to fire upon the three prisoners who had then just turned to face them. All three fell as a result of the volley. Captain Bowen-Colthurst left the yard and the firing party began to file out. . . .

40. "I [Bowen-Colthurst] had been busy on the previous evening up to about 3 am examining documents found on these three men and I recognised from these documents that these 3 men were all very dangerous characters. I, therefore, sent for an armed guard of six men and ordered them to load their rifles and keep their eyes on the prisoners. The guard room was full of men and was not a suitable place, in my opinion, in which to examine

prisoners. I ordered, therefore, the 3 prisoners to go into the small courtyard of the guard room. I regret now that I did not have these three men handcuffed and surrounded as the yard was a place from which they might have escaped. When I ordered these three men into the yard I did not, however, know this. The guard was some little distance from the prisoners and as I considered that there was a reasonable chance of the prisoners making their escape; and knowing the three prisoners, from correspondence captured on them the previous evening, to be dangerous characters, I called upon the guard to fire upon them, which they did with effect, the 3 men being killed. The documents found on these 3 men have been forwarded to the orderly room."

—Report of the Royal Commission into the arrest of Francis Sheehy Skeffingon, Mr. Thomas Dickson, and Mr. Patrick James McIntyre[45]

All over the city the strain was telling. In the various garrisons, morale was still strong, but a note of realism was creeping in. In the city center, things were becoming more precarious for the rebels as their garrisons came under relentless sniper and artillery fire.

By this point the center of Dublin was showing the signs of a city at war. Civilians were suffering from a shortage of food, there was no bread, roads were closed, and an increasing number of civilians had been shot by snipers or caught in crossfire. While many city residents, including most of the middle class and the separation women, were still hostile, the fact that the rebels were managing to hold out, and the courage with which they were doing so, was, however modestly, beginning to have an effect on some.

British troops in Trinity College.

Thursday, April 27

Fires raged all around the center of Dublin. A barrage of incendiary shells has set all of Lower Sackville Street ablaze. As he inspected one of the outposts, James Connolly was wounded in the ankle. He dragged himself back to the GPO, where he was placed on a stretcher. He dictated a manifesto to his secretary, Winifred Kearney, that he later read to the garrison. It was hopelessly optimistic.

In reality the GPO was surrounded and cut off from any hope of reinforcement or escape. With the fires caused by the incendiary shells drawing increasingly closer, even the most determined rebels in the GPO knew that those flames must soon engulf them.

In the South Dublin Union, fierce close-quarter fighting had intensified in the corridors and wards of the hospital, which now came under

Several civilians and looters have been killed. The foolhardiness of the looters—mostly women and children—is amazing. The Pro-Cathedral was only saved by a miracle from the fire. A change in the wind caused the fire to shift towards Earl Street. The priests had everything ready in bags for departure, including the parochial records.... Priests attending calls are in great danger. Fr. John O'Reilly had a narrow escape attending a Volunteer brought into Wynn's Hotel. Fr. Richard Bowden and a Dominican heard confessions in the G.P.O. for several hours yesterday [Wednesday].

—Monsignor M. Curran, P.P., witness statement[46]

renewed attack by troops coming from Kings-bridge. The Fourth Battalion under Ceannt and his second-in-command Cathal Brugha would experience some of the grimmest and bloodiest action of the Rising. More close-quarter fighting took place around the North King Street area. After two days in action against rebels from Ned Daly's Four Courts garrison, the Second Battalion South Staffordshires had lost five officers and forty-two men. This area saw some of the worst civilian casualties when British troops shot dead fifteen unarmed civilians as they attempted to clear the houses of rebel fighters.

We had now reached Thursday, April 27. The quadrangles presented an extraordinary appearance. Some 4,000 troops were stationed in the College. Horses tied to the chains which enclosed the grass plots gave the place the appearance of a vast open-air stable or horse fair. Men stood in ranks or sprawled on the pavements or on the doorsteps—anywhere—sometimes closely packed and fast asleep in every conceivable attitude. Many of them had put in a hard night's work. A large number were of the Sherwood Foresters and of the South Stafford-shire Territorials. Many of these men were very young, and most of them had but recently joined the colours. Looking now at their sleeping forms and tired faces, one must remember that the work of rounding up and hunting down the Rebels is not only arduous, it is in the highest degree dangerous. Not a few of the officers and men who had been through these nocturnal and diurnal operations told me that they would prefer to be at the Front. At the Front, they said, you know the direction from which you may expect a bullet. Here the enemy is all around you. He lurks in dark passages and among chimney stacks, and when at last you think you have hunted him down, you find yourself in possession of a peaceful citizen who gives some plausible reason for his presence. That these young fellows should be wearied after their night of peril and strenuous exertion was not to be wondered at.

—John Joly,
Trinity College garrison[47]

opposite left: Burning buildings in Sackville Street.

opposite right: Winifred Kearney.

British troops in military truck.

top: Irish Volunteers inside the GPO.

bottom: British soldiers at barricade.

This night also was calm and beautiful, but this night was the most sinister and woeful of those that have passed. The sound of artillery, of rifles, machine guns, grenades did not cease even for a moment. From my window I saw a red flare that crept to the sky, and stole over it and remained there glaring, the smoke reached from the ground to the clouds, and I could see great red sparks go soaring to enormous heights; while always, in the calm air, hour after hour there was buzzing and rattling and thudding of guns, and, but for the guns, silence.

It is in a dead silence this Insurrection is being fought, and one imagines what must be the feeling of these men, young for the most part, and unused to violence, who are submitting silently to the crash and flame and explosion by which they are surrounded.

—James Stephens[49]

Suddenly some oil works near Abbey Street are singed by the conflagration, and immediately a solid sheet of blinding death-white flame rushes hundreds of feet into the air with a thunderous explosion which shakes the walls. It is followed by a heavy bombardment as hundred of drums of oil explode. The intense light compels one to close the eyes. Even here the heat is so terrible that it strikes one like a solid thing as blast and scorching air come in through the glassless windows. Millions of sparks are floating in masses for hundred of yards around O'Connell Street and as a precaution we were ordered to drench the barricades with water again. The whole thing seems too terrible to be real. Crimson-tinged men moved around dazedly. Above us all the sharp crack of rifle fire predominates, while the deadly rattle of the machine gun sounds like the coughing laughter of jeering spirits.

. . . Inside the central telegraph room which runs along the entire length of the GPO the men stand silently at their posts, black and bronze statues against the terrible glow of the sky. Un-awed and undaunted, their gaze ever fixed on the glistening cobbles and the shadowed lanes whence all attacks must be directed, they wait expectantly. Now and again the flames beat upwards in a flash of light that reveals every detail behind the barriers. Then they subside as suddenly and lines of black shadow, rays of darkness as it were, creep over us. Fortunately the wind is blowing seawards, the myriads of blazing fragments are carried away from the GPO. Glowing sparks however now begin to shower down with a pattering sound like soft rain and threaten to set everything on fire.

—Dick Humphries,
GPO garrison[50]

The heat from the burning block opposite the GPO was beyond belief. Despite the great width of O'Connell Street the sacks, etc. in the windows began to scorch and show signs of smoldering. Batches of men had to be hastily formed to continually drench the window fortifications with water. Dense volumes of acrid smoke, myriads of sparks and splinters of falling debris were being blown to the GPO by a strong north-east wind. Lurid flames leapt skywards and the spectacle in the gathering darkness could only be likened to Dante's Inferno. The intensity of the heat grew steadily worse and the water being poured from buckets and hoses was converted into steam as it touched the fortifications. There had to be a withdrawal from the front of the building of all save those who were combating the risk of a conflagration in the Post Office itself. Our struggle with this new danger seemed to go on for interminable hours. The men were soot-stained, steam-scalded and fire-scorched, sweating, weary and parched.

—Michael Staines,
GPO garrison[51]

Friday, April 28

EARLY ON FRIDAY MORNING SIR JOHN Grenfell Maxwell sailed into Dublin. He had been appointed Commander-in-Chief of all British troops in Ireland. Maxwell continued Lowe's strategy of squeezing rebel positions. Conditions in the GPO were deteriorating as heavy shelling increased and the fires spread up Sackville Street. Flames would soon engulf the GPO. The rebels' position looked impossible. By 6:00 pm on Friday it was clear that they would have to surrender or attempt a breakout and try to join up with the Four Courts garrison. At 8:00 they attempted to do so. While the main body of the GPO garrison managed to get to the safety of some houses in nearby Moore Street, The O'Rahilly was killed as he attempted to cross the street with his men.

General Sir John Maxwell.

Headquarters, Army of the Irish Republic,
General Post Office, Dublin
28th April 1916 9.30 a.m.
The forces of the Irish Republic which was proclaimed in Dublin on Easter Monday, 24th April, have been in possession of the central part of the Capital since 12 noon on that day. . . . During the course of yesterday afternoon and evening the enemy succeeded in cutting our communications with our other positions in the city and Headquarters is today isolated.

The enemy has burnt down whole blocks of houses, apparently with the object of giving themselves a clear field for the play of artillery and field guns against us. We have been bombarded during the evening and night by shrapnel and machine gun fire, but without material damage to our position, which is of great strength.

We are busy completing arrangements for the final defense of Headquarters, and are determined to hold it while the building lasts.

I desire now, lest I may not have an opportunity later, to pay homage to the gallantry of the soldiers of Irish Freedom who have during the past four days been writing with fire and steel the most glorious chapter in the later history of Ireland. Justice can never be done to their heroism, to their discipline, to their gay and unconquerable spirit in the midst of peril and death.

Let me, who have led them into this, speak, in my own, and in my fellow-commanders' names, and in the name of Ireland, present and to come, their praise, and ask them who come after them to remember them.

For four days they have fought and toiled, almost without cessation, almost without sleep, and in the intervals of fighting they have sung songs of the freedom of Ireland. No man has complained, no man has asked 'Why?'

Each individual has spent himself, happy to pour out his strength for Ireland and for freedom. If they do not win this fight, they will, at least,

have deserved to win it. But win it they will, although they may win it in death. Already they have won a great thing. They have redeemed Dublin from many shames and made her name splendid among the names of cities.

If I were to mention names of individuals, my list would be a long one. I will name only that of Commandant-General James Connolly, commanding the Dublin Division. He lies wounded, but is still the guiding brain of our resistance.

If we accomplish no more than we have accomplished, I am satisfied. I am satisfied that we have saved Ireland's honour. I am satisfied that we should have accomplished the task of enthroning, as well as proclaiming, the Irish Republic as a sovereign State, had our arrangements for a simultaneous rising of the whole country, with a combined plan as sound as the Dublin plan has been proved to be, been allowed to go through on Easter Sunday.

Of the fatal countermanding order which prevented these plans from being carried out I shall not speak further. Both Eoin MacNeill and we have acted in the best interests of Ireland.

For my part, as to anything I have done in this, I am not afraid to face either the judgment of God or the judgment of posterity.

(signed) P. H. Pearse
Commandant-General
Commanding-in-Chief,
the Army of the Irish Republic
President of the
Provisional Government[52]

Army of the Irish Republic,
(Dublin Command)
Headquarters, April 28th, 1916
To Soldiers,
. . . Courage, boys, we are winning
and in the hour of victory let us not
forget the splendid women who have
everywhere stood by us and cheered
us on. Never had man or woman a
grander cause. Never was a cause
more grandly served.
—James Connolly, GPO[53]

left: The O'Rahilly in full Volunteer uniform,
ca. 1915.

above: The O'Rahilly and his wife,
Nancy, ca. 1912.

From the sea it looks as if the entire center of Dublin was in flames ... when we got to North Wall, bullets were flying about, the crackle of musketry and machine gun fire breaking out every other minute but from what I can gather the nerve center of the movement is in Dublin and in that part we have surrounded. . . . I think the signs are that the rebels have had enough. I will know for certain tonight.

—General Sir John Maxwell,
letter to his wife,
Friday morning[54]

This morning there are no newspapers, no bread, no milk, no news. The sun is shining, and the streets are lively but discreet. All people continue to talk to one another without distinction of class, but nobody knows what any person thinks.

—James Stephens[55]

You can have no idea of what it was like. The rebels had cut all communications, & if they had cut the wire to the Curragh which thanks be to God was the only one left untouched we [could] never have got the troops up & I think the game [would] have been up. . . . Meanwhile the situation is very serious indeed. The rebels are in houses, to shoot at the troops so as to effectually prevent them from coping with things. . . . But it can only be a matter of days—street fighting is more difficult to cope with than any other form. Meanwhile there is loss of life and great general suffering & want. We are now heavily guarded here & unless unforeseen complications arise should be all right.

—Letter from
Lady Alice Wimborne
to her mother,
from the Vice-Regal Lodge,
April 28[56]

Many people have taken refuge in the Pro-Cathedral. People entering or leaving are shot at by the military. Under these circumstances, the administrator applied to the military that they should occupy it. This they did, in great force, later in the day. They occupy both Church and Presbytery [and] . . . Tyrone House, the Model schools. They also stated that they might have to send there the guests in the Hammam and Gresham Hotels. . . .

Whole districts are without provisions—milk, butter, bread or meat. Only for flour, many would be very badly off.

—Monsignor M. Curran, P.P.,
witness statement[57]

Written after I was shot. Darling Nancy I was shot leading a rush up Moore St and took refuge in a doorway. While I was there I heard the men pointing out where I was and made a bolt for the laneway I am now in. I got more [than] one bullet, I think. Tons and tons of love dearie to you and the boys and to Nell and Anna. It was a good fight anyhow. Please deliver this to Nannie O'Rahilly, 40 Herbert Park, Dublin. Goodbye Darling.

—The O'Rahilly's note
to his wife and family,
found on his body
after his death[58]

Saturday, April 29

Under unbearable pressure and with no possible or probable escape in sight, Pearse was forced to consider surrender. He sent Nurse Elizabeth O'Farrell, a member of Cumann na mBan, to the British to seek terms. The answer came back: there would be no terms offered. The British would

Elizabeth O'Farrell in her nurse's uniform.

At 12.30 pm information came that a Sinn Fein nurse—Miss Elizabeth O'Farrell—was waiting at the Parnell monument. She had been sent by Commander General Pearse to negotiate terms of surrender. General Lowe ordered me to accompany him. . . .

In peacetime the journey from Park Gate Street to our destination, the shop at the Parnell monument, would have been a matter of mere minutes. We took a zig-zag course in and out of side streets, taking the intervening corners at high speed to dodge the sharpshooters who were posted at vantage points on the roofs of the houses.

Two bullets did get the panel of the near door of the car which was an official saloon supplied for the use of staff. Owing to the skilful driver and the speed, I do not expect the snipers realised who were in it until it had skidded round the next corner. Eventually we arrived at a small newsagent's shop a few doors from the corner of Great Britain Street, where it joins Upper Sackville Street at the Parnell monument.

The general communicated the terms to Nurse O'Farrell and she

was allowed half an hour to return with the reply of Commandant General Pearse, who was in command at the rear of the GPO and controlled Moore Street and the adjoining thoroughfares. Upper Sackville was still swept by snipers and while waiting for the return of the nurse, General Lowe, who was in his staff uniform and a very conspicuous mark, strolled the Sackville Street to note the position.

As the whole of Upper and Lower Sackville Street was held by the rebels at this time, and I felt responsible for the general's safety, I pointed out that he would draw the fire on himself if spotted. He made little of it, but in the end I persuaded him to return to the newsagent's shop, and wait there for the dispatches from Commandant General Pearse.

Soon after the nurse returned with a reply imposing conditionals. These were refused, and the general sent her back again to say that only unconditional surrender would be accepted. She was given half an hour to return with the reply.

—Captain Harry De Courcy-Wheeler, staff captain to General Lowe[59]

accept nothing but an unconditional surrender. Pearse and Connolly reluctantly agreed. Having been interviewed by General Sir John Maxwell, Pádraig Pearse signed the order of surrender at 3:45 pm.

After the surrender, the garrison from the GPO and the nearby Four Courts garrison under Ned Daly were kept overnight at the top of Sackville Street in the grass plot in front of the Rotunda Hospital, ringed in by soldiers with bayonets. The space would have held 150 comfortably. That night there were 450. Conditions were terrible, with no toilet facilities provided, and there were allegations of ill treatment. Among the prisoners were Tom Clarke and Seán Mac Diarmada, both of whom were singled out for special treatment. Another Irish Volunteer kept overnight at the Rotunda was Michael Collins, who had been aide-de-camp to Joseph Plunkett in the GPO. He would later exact a heavy price from the British for the defeat of the Rising.

That night, as the rain fell on the prisoners, the tricolor still continued to fly over the now-smoldering ruins of the GPO. The next morning the prisoners were marched to Richmond Barracks.

1.40 p.m. 29 April
A woman has come in and tells me you wish to negotiate with me. I am prepared to receive you in Britain Street at the north end of Moore Street, provided that you surrender unconditionally. You will proceed up Moore Street, accompanied only by the woman who brings you this note under a white flag.

—General Lowe's first note to Pearse [60]

Pádraig Pearse surrenders to General Lowe. Nurse Elizabeth O'Farrell is standing out of sight to the right of Pearse.

HQ [Headquarters] Moore Street
Believing that the glorious stand which has been made by the soldiers of Irish freedom during the past five days in Dublin has been sufficient to gain recognition of Ireland's national claim at an international peace conference, and desirous of preventing further slaughter of the civilian population, and to save the lives of as many people as possible of our followings, the Members of the Provisional Government here present have agreed by a majority to open negotiations with the British commander.
P. H. Pearse,
Commandant General,
Commanding in Chief,
Army of the Irish Republic.
29th April 1914

—text of Pearse's handwritten surrender, written on a sheet of cardboard[61]

2.00 p.m. 29 April
I have received your letter. Nothing can be considered until you surrender unconditionally or you surrender to me. I will take steps to give everyone under your orders sufficient time to surrender before I recommence hostilities which I have temporarily suspended.

—General Lowe's response to Pearse[62]

At 2.30 pm Commander General Pearse surrendered to General Lowe accompanied by myself and Lieutenant Lowe at the junction of Moore Street and Great Britain Street. He handed over his arms and military equipment. His sword and automatic repeating pistol in holster with pouch of ammunition, and his canteen . . . were handed to me. . . .

Two Army official cars were waiting. Commandant General Pearse, accompanied by Lieut. Lowe, was driven in the general's car, proceeded by the general and myself in the other car. We drove to headquarters, Irish Command, to interview General Sir John Maxwell, the British Commander-in-Chief. After the interview, Commandant Pearse signed several typed copies of a manifesto, which was dated by himself, Dublin 29th April 1916. . . .

After signing these documents Commandant General Pearse was conducted to a sitting room at headquarters.

I was ordered to keep guard over him and was locked in a room alone with him. I was handed a loaded revolver with orders to keep it pointed at Commandant Pearse, and to shoot should he make an effort to escape. This was a very responsible and serious order to obey and to carry out should it have become necessary.

—Captain De Courcy-Wheeler[63]

In order to prevent the further slaughter of Dublin citizens, and in the hope of saving the lives of our followers now surrounded and hopelessly outnumbered, the members of the Provisional Government present at Head Quarters have agreed to an unconditional Surrender and the Commandants of the various districts in the City and country will order their commands to lay down arms.

P. H. Pearse
29th April 1916
Dublin

—Text of Pearse's typed surrender [64]

I agree to these conditions for the men only under my own command in the Moore Street district, and for the men in the Stephen's Green Command.
James Connolly
April 29 1916

—Text of Connolly's handwritten note [65]

And eventually somebody came to us and told us that Pearse had sent out an envoy to negotiate with the British. About an hour and a half to two hours later we were all told to march out onto Moore Street. . . . We get out onto this lane and as we went out onto the backyard of the house, Sean McDermott, one of the leaders, addressed us and told us, "this is only the beginning of the fight. All the leaders would be executed but it's up to you men to carry it on." We filed up to Moore Street, we're lined up there in fours. We're marched right up to O'Connell Street, we're formed into two lines on each side of the street, we march up to the front and drop our ammunition, went back to our original positions on each side of the street, and officers with notebooks came down and took down our names. A funny incident happened there. They came along past me, and about 3 men down the officer looked at a fellow, wrote down his name and walked on. So when he had walked down a certain distance one of the men asked, "Did that officer know you?" and the man replied, "That's my brother." When that formality was over we were marched again into a little patch of green in front of the rotunda, and we were all made to lay down there and anyone who put his foot out on the gravel got a whack of the whip. We stayed out there all night. In the middle of the night one of the British officers, as a way of amusing himself, took out the leaders, he took out poor old Tom Clarke and stripped him to the bum, and made all kinds of discouraging remarks about him, saying, "This old man has been out of it before, he has a shop across the street there." And he took several others out there, and that officer's name was Lee Wilson. He was subsequently shot by the IRA.

—Joe Sweeney, GPO garrison [66]

James Connolly lies on a stretcher following the surrender.

Rebel soldier marched over O'Connell Bridge.

Sunday, April 30

As the prisoners from the GPO were marched off from the Rotunda, Nurse Elizabeth O'Farrell, who had been the go-between in the dealings between Pearse and General Lowe the previous day, was again called upon, this time by the British. She accompanied Lowe's staff captain, Captain Harry De Courcy-Wheeler, to deliver the letter of surrender to the rest of the Dublin garrisons. The initial reaction was one of disbelief and grief. At 12:00 noon, De Courcy-Wheeler received the surrender of Mallin, Markievicz, and the College of Surgeons' garrison, which consisted of 109 men and 10 women. As it happened, Countess Markievicz was a cousin of De Courcy-Wheeler's wife.

The next rebel garrison on the list was Boland's Mill, under the command of de Valera, who refused to surrender until he had heard from Thomas MacDonagh, the commandant in Jacob's Biscuit Factory. MacDonagh was allowed to go to Éamonn Ceannt at the South Dublin Union and his

left: Committal shots of Countess Markievicz taken after her arrest.

above: Michael Mallin and Countess Markievicz after their surrender.

That night I received orders from the General to be at the bank at the corner of Rutland Square and Upper Sackville Street at 8 am the following morning, Sunday April 30, 1916, to meet Nurse Elizabeth O'Farrell—known to the British Army as the "Sinn Fein Nurse"—who had undertaken to conduct me to the headquarters of the various commands in and around the city for the purpose of communicating the surrender orders.

A military car—No. R1 4064—was waiting, driven by one of the Royal Army Service Corps drivers, with the sergeant major of the 5th Royal Irish Regiment as escort. I was unarmed, Nurse O'Farrell carried an old white apron on a stick as a flag of truce, and she and I sat behind.

I decide to go first to the College of Surgeons, Stephen's Green, which was strongly held by the rebels and which was keeping up a continuous fusillade with the British garrison in the United Service Club and the Shelbourne Hotel. On the way I had, by the general's instructions, ordered an escort of military to be in readiness at Trinity College to take over the College of Surgeons if the rebels surrendered. At Lambert Brien's shop in Grafton Street my motor was brought to a standstill by the crossfiring, and I decided to allow the nurse to proceed alone and deliver the document at the college under cover of the white flag. Both she and it would be recognised and respected. She returned at about 9.30 having delivered the message.

—Captain De Courcy-Wheeler [67]

I had to walk from there [Grafton Street] to the College of Surgeons with a white flag. Bullets were whistling round Stephen's Green. There was no one on the streets and I saw no dead or wounded. I got in at the side door in York Street and asked for Commandant Mallin and was told he was sleeping and that Countess Markievicz was next in command. I saw her and gave her the order—she was very much surprised and she went to discuss it with Commandant Mallin, whom I afterwards saw. I gave her a slip with the directions as to how to surrender—the Southern sides being ordered to surrender at St. Patrick's Park. I don't think this was carried out and I don't know where the College of Surgeons' troops did ultimately surrender. I left and went back to Grafton Street to Captain Wheeler.

—Nurse Elizabeth O'Farrell [68]

May 1st 11.00 am
I had no time to continue this yesterday, but during the afternoon three of the rebel strongholds surrendered—Jacob's, Boland's, and the College of Surgeons on St. Stephen's Green. From this last building 160 men surrendered and were marched down Grafton Street. It is said that among them was Countess Markievicz, dressed in a man's uniform. It is also said that the military made her take down the green republican flag flying over the building herself and replace it with a white one: when she surrendered she took off her bandolier and kissed it and her revolver before handing them to the officer. She has been one of the most dangerous of the leaders, and I hope will be treated with the same severity as the men. People who saw them marched down Grafton Street said they held themselves erect, and looked absolutely defiant!

—Lady Norway [69]

Fr. Augustine Hayden, OFM Cap.

outpost at Jameson's Distillery. They were accompanied by two Capuchin priests sympathetic to the rebels, Fr. Aloysius and Fr. Augustine. The area surrounding the two garrisons was still heavily defended by rebels. Despite misgivings, particularly those of Ceannt in the South Dublin Union, all remaining garrisons surrendered.

Thence I endeavoured to drive her to Boland's Mill, Ringsend. Owing to the barricades across Lower Mount Street, and having tried all the routes down by the river which were held by the rebels, and hearing reports of continuous firing further on, I had again to allow the nurse to proceed on foot to deliver the document under cover of the white flag.

Boland's Mill, commanded by Éamon de Valera, was a seemingly impregnable fortress. De Valera had avoided shells from the naval reserve boat Helga, firing from the River Liffey, by the simple ruse of hoisting his flag on a building some distance from the mill. British soldiers encircling the mill shouted and waved their rifles at Nurse O'Farrell as she made her way towards it. She waved her white flag back at them and went on. Volunteers lifted her through a window into a small room. There she came face to face with Commandant de Valera, who was ghostlike with his uniform spattered with flour from the bakery. He said: 'My immediate superior officer is Commandant MacDonagh. I will take orders only from him.'

The nurse made her way back to the captain's car.

I took her up again and drove her through the Castle, up Ship Street to St. Patrick's Park, being the nearest point that the motor could approach to Jacob's Factory as this and the surrounding neighbourhood was very strongly held by the rebels. I was to meet her again at 12 noon. These visits were for the purpose of handing in the orders to surrender to the various commandants, not to receive their surrenders.

Nurse O'Farrell was very intimate with the situation of all these command posts and had no difficulty in directing the motor on the best route to take and where to go next, so that no time was lost.

To reach Jacob's biscuit factory, now a high, embattled fortress, Miss O'Farrell had walked through a maze of streets which were a death trap to the troops. From its two towers vigilant Volunteers had a magnificent view of the whole city. Its lofty windows dominated even Dublin Castle—the city's administrative centre.

The strength of its garrison was 150 men, some boys of the Fianna Eireann, the Republican Boy Scout movement, and a part of Cumann na mBan, the women's wing of the freedom movement to which Miss O'Farrell belonged. The commander of this stronghold whom she now sought was Commandant Thomas MacDonagh.

Near the factory Miss O'Farrell, with her white flag resting on her shoulder, asked for him. There was a whispered conversation among the Volunteers and a large white bandage was produced. 'We will take you to him, but you will have to be blindfolded,' she was told.

She was led along streets for a few minutes and eventually heard and recognised the commandant's voice. The bandage was removed from her eyes. She handed over the typewritten surrender manifesto, which Padraig Pearse and James Connolly had signed. Commandant MacDonagh, his face grave, declared first that he would not take orders from a prisoner.

'I will not surrender myself,' he said, 'until I have spoken with General Lowe, my brother officers who are already prisoners, and the officers under my command.'

—Captain De Courcy-Wheeler[70]

Fr. Aloysius Travers, OFM Cap.

On consultation with Commandant Ceannt and other officers. I have decided to agree to unconditional surrender also.

Thomas Mac Donagh
Commandant
30 IV 1916

—Text of Thomas MacDonagh's handwritten note[71]

They did not arrive and I began to wonder what was causing the delay. In about 15 minutes, however, we saw the South Dublin Union Garrison marching in, and at once my eye caught sight of the figure of the leader.

The whole column marched splendidly with guns slung from their left shoulders and their hands swinging freely at their sides. They wore no look of defeat, but rather of victory. It seemed they had come out to celebrate a triumph and were marching to receive a decoration. Ceannt was in the middle of the front [row] with one man on either side. But my eyes were riveted on him so tall was his form, so noble was his bearing, and so manly his stride. He was indeed the worthy captain of a brave band who had fought a clean fight for Ireland.

They drew up just opposite us as we stood at the corner where [Bride] Street meets [Ross] street and grounded their guns at his command. Father Aloysius and myself looked on in silence. We saw Éamonn give up his gun and then his belt to an English officer. But when I saw them take his Volunteer uniform I said to Father Aloysius: 'I can't stand this any longer. Come along and we'll let them see what we think of those men.' We walked across the street, shook hands warmly with Éamonn and with a 'Goodbye and God bless you' just looked at the officers and departed for Church Street after a tense and trying day.

—Father Augustine,
Capuchin priest,
witness statement[72]

Monday, May 1

SPORADIC RESISTANCE CONTINUED FOR A DAY or two, but by Monday all major rebel garrisons had surrendered. The military danger had passed.

It was all over. The Rising had been defeated, but the rebels had managed to hold out for a week against vastly superior odds. As the leaders and men and women under their command were led off in the custody of the British, booed by certain sections of the Dublin populace, it seemed like an ignominious end. Time, however, would tell a different story. From the jaws of defeat, the rebels were about to effect a remarkable change.

Prisoners under escort pass by ruins, May 1916.

PART THREE

When Myth
and History
Rhyme

Aftermath

The Rising had left Dublin city center in ruins. The destruction was unparalleled and comparable to anything seen in the war-torn towns and cities of France and Belgium. The human cost was over five hundred people killed during the events of the week. Of those who lost their lives, more than half were civilians. Of those civilian casualties, more than fifty were children. One hundred and seventeen British officers and men were killed, as were fifty-nine rebels.

May 1st, 2.00pm
Today for the first time since Easter Monday the *Irish Times* issued a paper with news of the rebellion....

Today's paper bears the dates "Friday, Saturday, and Monday, April 28th, 29th, and May 1st"—an incident unique, I should think, in the history of the paper.

It contains the various proclamations in full, which I will cut out and send to you. Please keep them, as they will be of interest in the future.

The paper states that Sir R. Casement is a prisoner in the Tower. So he was not shot without trial, as we were told. It also gives a list of the large shops and business establishments that have been destroyed—a total of 146.

—Lady Norway[1]

left: Destroyed buildings in Lower Abbey Street after the Rising.

opposite: The burnt-out ruins of the Dublin Bread Company.

Although the fighting was over, the casualties of Easter Week were not. The leaders still remained to be dealt with. They did not have long to wait. Pádraig Pearse was under no illusion as to his likely fate. He had, however, hopes that the lives of his followers would be spared. In his cell at Arbour Hill Prison, Pearse wrote a number of poems, two for his mother and one, "To My Brother," dedicated to Willie, his younger sibling who had worked with him at St Enda's and was with him

Arbour Hill Barracks
1st May 1916
My dear Mother,
You will, I know, have been longing to hear from me. I do not know how much you have heard since the last note I sent you from the GPO....

Our hope and belief is that the Government will spare the lives of our followers, but we do not expect that they will save the lives of the leaders. We are ready to die and we shall die cheerfully and proudly. Personally I do not hope or even desire to live but I do hope and desire and believe that the lives of all our followers will be saved including the lives dear to you and me (my own excepted) and this will be a great consolation to me when dying.

You must not grieve for all this. We have preserved Ireland's honour and our own. Our deeds of last week are the most splendid in Ireland's history. People will say hard things of us now, but we shall be remembered by posterity and blessed by unborn generations. You too will be blessed because you were my mother....

Love to W. W., M.B., Miss Byrne and your own dear self

P

— Pádraig Pearse's letter to his mother, never delivered but used against him at his court-martial[2]

in the GPO. As is clear from the letter to his mother following his arrest, he believed that Willie's life was safe because he had no leadership role in the Rising. The letter was never delivered but was instead given to Sir John Maxwell and used against Pearse at his court-martial.

Maxwell was in no mood for mercy. Procedures were drawn up for military courts-martial to try rebel leaders and for execution by firing squad in the event of guilty verdicts. There was little doubt but that executions would take place.

To My Brother

O faithful!
Moulded in one womb
We two have stood together all the
    years
All the glad years and all the sorrow-
    ful years,
Own brothers; through good repute
    and ill,
In direct peril true to me,
Leaving all things for me, spending
    yourself
in the hard service that I taught to you,
of all the men I have known on earth,
you only have been my familiar friend
Nor needed I another.
    —Pádraig Pearse, written in his
    cell in Arbour Hill, May 1, 1916[3]

left: Dublin firemen at work in the rubble.

opposite: The inside of the GPO after the fires.

Paying the Price:
Courts-Martial and Executions

PEARSE, ON MAY 2, WAS THE FIRST TO FACE court-martial. He was Prisoner Number 1. While three witnesses were called by the prosecution, Pearse called no witnesses in his defense but, in the tradition of earlier Irish rebel leaders, did make a statement, his "speech from the dock."

Maxwell confirmed the guilty verdict within hours and signed the warrant. That same day Thomas Clarke and Thomas MacDonagh were also court-martialed. They, too, were found guilty and sentenced to death.

All three men, Pearse, Clarke, and MacDonagh, were transferred to Kilmainham Gaol that evening. They were held in separate cells and informed that they would be shot at dawn. All three condemned prisoners were attended by priests, who gave them the sacraments.

During his final hours, Pearse wrote again to his mother and wrote his final poem, "The Wayfarer." MacDonagh, also in a cell in Kilmainham awaiting his execution, took the opportunity to write to his wife, Muriel.

To: Major-General A. E. Sandbach, GOC troops, Dublin
From: Brigadier J. Young, Headquarters, Irish Command
2nd May 1916
In the event of any of the Sinn Fein prisoners being condemned to death today, they will be segregated (so far as circumstances permit) and asked whether they want to see relatives or friends or chaplains; and these persons will be sent for as required by the prisoners. A number of motorcars will be stationed at Richmond Barracks for this purpose, and more may be asked for from HQ, Irish Command, as necessary. The whole of the visitors and friends are to be taken back to their homes before 3.30 am the next day, at which time the first firing party will parade. The first man to be shot will be brought out at 3.45 am facing the firing party officer, and 12 men at 10 paces distant. The rifles of the firing party will be loaded by other men behind their backs, one rifle with a blank cartridge, and eleven with ball, and the firing party will be told that this is the arrangement, and no man is to know which rifle is loaded with blank. There will be 4 Firing Parties, who will fire in turn.

—Text of memorandum sent from Irish Command HQ[4]

Illustrated portrait of Pádraig Pearse.

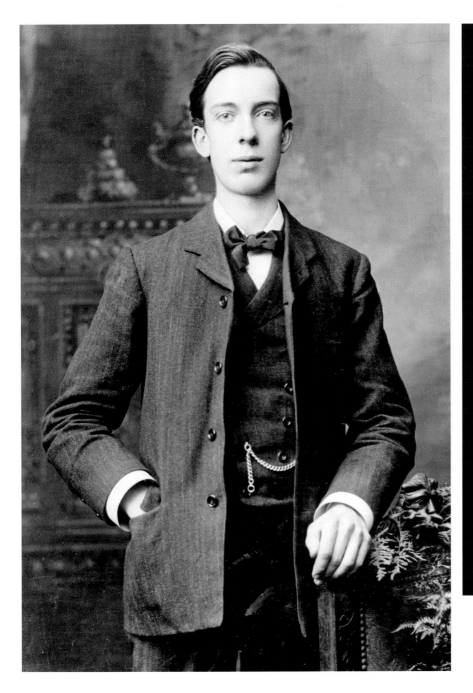

My object in agreeing to an unconditional surrender was to prevent the further slaughter of the civil population of Dublin and to save the lives of our gallant followers who, having made for six days a stand unparalleled in military history, were now surrounded and (in the case of those under the immediate command of Headquarters) without food. I fully understand now, as then, that my own life is forfeit to British law, and I shall die very cheerfully if I can think that the British Government, as it has already shown itself strong, will now show itself magnanimous enough to accept my single life in forfeiture and give a general amnesty to the brave men and boys who fought at my bidding.... When I was a child of ten I went down on my bare knees by my bedside one night and promised God that I should devote my life to an effort to free my country. I have kept that promise ... we went into the fight. I am glad we did. We seem to have lost. We have not lost. To refuse to fight would have been to lose; to fight is to win. We have kept faith with the past, and handed on a tradition to the future.... I assume I am speaking to Englishmen, who value their freedom and who profess to be fighting for the freedom of Belgium and Serbia. Believe, that we, too, love freedom and desire it. To us it is more desirable than anything in the world. If you strike us down now, we shall rise again and renew the fight. You cannot conquer Ireland. You cannot extinguish the Irish passion for freedom. If our deed has not been sufficient to win freedom, then our children will win it by a better deed.

—Pádraig Pearse, Kilmainham Gaol, probably written between midnight May 2 and his execution early on May 3[5]

Willie Pearse, ca. 1914/1915.
He was executed on May 4.

top: Pádraig and Willie Pearse talking, ca. 1915.

bottom: Mrs. Margaret Pearse, mother of Pádraig and Willie.

TRIAL OF P.H. PEARSE
PRISONER NUMBER ONE
DATE: 2 May 1916
LOCATION: Richmond Barracks
JUDGES: Brigadier General C.G. Blackader (President), Lieutenant Colonel G. German, Lieutenant Colonel W.J. Kent
CHARGE: Did an act to wit did take part in an armed rebellion and in the waging of war against His Majesty the King, such act being of such a nature as to be calculated to be prejudicial to the Defence of the Realm and being done with the intention and for the purpose of assisting the enemy.
PLEA: Not guilty
VERDICT: Guilty. Death by being shot

—From the official schedule of Pearse's court-martial[6]

I have just done one of the hardest things I have ever had to do. I have had to condemn to death one of the finest characters I have ever come across. There must be something very wrong in the state of things that makes a man like that a rebel. I don't wonder his pupils adored him.

—Comment about Pádraig Pearse made by Brigadier General Blackader to the Countess of Fingall at dinner after Pearse's court-martial and death sentence[7]

May 3
My dearest Mother,
. . . I have just received Holy Communion. I am happy except for the great grief of parting from you. This is the death I should have asked for if God had given me the choice of all deaths—to die a soldier's death for Ireland and for freedom.

We have done all right. People will say hard things of us now, but later, they will praise us. Do not grieve for all this, but think of it as a sacrifice which God asked of me and of you.

Good-bye again dear Mother. May God bless you for your great love for me and for your great faith, and may He remember all that you have so bravely suffered. I hope soon to see Papa, and in a little while we shall all be together again.

Wow-wow [Margaret, his sister], Willie, Mary Brigid, and Mother, goodbye. I have not words to tell my love of you, and how my heart yearns to [sic] you all. I will call to you in my heart at the last moment. Your son
Pat

—Pádraig Pearse, written shortly before his execution[8]

Thomas MacDonagh, his wife, Muriel, and baby son, Donagh. MacDonagh was executed on May 3.

TRIAL OF THOMAS MACDONAGH
PRISONER NUMBER THIRTY
DATE: 2 May 1916
LOCATION: Richmond Barracks
JUDGES: Brigadier General C.G. Blackader (President), Lieutenant Colonel G. German, Lieutenant Colonel W. J. Kent
CHARGE: Did an act to wit did take part in an armed rebellion and in the waging of war against His Majesty the King, such act being of such a nature as to be calculated to be prejudicial to the Defence of the Realm and being done with the intention and for the purpose of assisting the enemy.
PLEA: Not guilty
VERDICT: Guilty. Death by being shot

—From the official schedule of the court-martial of Thomas MacDonagh[9]

Kilmainham Gaol
I, Thomas MacDonagh, having now heard the sentence of the court martial passed on me today declare that in all of the acts for which I have been arraigned, I have been actuated by one motive only, the love of my country, my desire to make her a sovereign independent state. I hope and pray that my acts will bring her lasting freedom and happiness. I am to die at dawn. I am ready to die, and I thank God that I die in so holy a cause. The one bitterness that death has for me is the separation it brings from my beloved wife Muriel, and from my children, Donagh and Barbara. God help and support them. Never was there a better woman than my wife, Muriel, or more adorable children than Don and Barbara. It breaks my heart to think I shall never see them again. But I have not wept or mourned. I counted the cost of this and am ready to pay the price. Muriel has been sent for. I do not know if she can come. She may have no one to take the children while she is coming. Assistance has been guaranteed from funds in the hands of Cumann na mBan to assist my family. My wife and I have given all for Ireland. Don my little boy remember me kindly and God bless you, Barbara. I loved you more than a child has ever been loved. Goodbye my love till we meet again in heaven.

—Thomas MacDonagh, May 2, 1916[10]

The prisoners had been informed that their families had been sent for and that they would be allowed one last visit. Because of continuing sporadic shooting, which delayed communications, neither the Pearse family nor Muriel MacDonagh received the news in time to get to the prison. Tom Clarke's wife, however, managed to get there in time. Kathleen Clarke was herself a prisoner in Dublin Castle, having been arrested the day before. She was taken under armed escort to Kilmainham, where she had her last meeting with her husband.

TRIAL OF THOMAS CLARKE
PRISONER NUMBER THIRTY-ONE
DATE: 2 May 1916
LOCATION: Richmond Barracks
JUDGES: Brigadier General C.G. Blackader (President), Lieutenant Colonel G. German, Lieutenant Colonel W. J. Kent
CHARGE: Did an act to wit did take part in an armed rebellion and in the waging of war against His Majesty the King, such act being of such a nature as to be calculated to be prejudicial to the Defence of the Realm and being done with the intention and for the purpose of assisting the enemy.
PLEA: Not guilty
VERDICT: Guilty. Death by being shot

—From the official schedule of the court-martial of Tom Clarke[11]

An officer came and said I had permission to see my husband. 'My God, Kathleen,' said one of the girls, 'what does that mean?' 'It means death.' 'Oh no,' said the girl; Marie Perolz was her name [a member of the Citizen Army]. 'Look,' said I, '[do you think] that if the British government were going to send my husband on a journey any shorter than to the next world that they'd get an officer and car out at midnight to go for me?' 'You're a stone,' said the girl. I was.

. . . Kilmainham was terrible. The conditions! There was a monk downstairs. He told me that my husband had put him out of the cell. There was no light in it, only a candle that a soldier held. 'Why did you surrender?', I asked Tom, 'I thought you were going to hold out for six months.' 'I wanted to,' he said, 'but the vote went against me.' We talked about the future the whole time. I never saw him so buoyed up. He said that the first blow had been struck and Ireland would get her freedom but that she'd have to go through hell first. I didn't cry. He had to face the ordeal by himself in the morning. If I broke down it might have broken him down. . . . I was expecting a baby but didn't tell him that in case it might upset him.

—Kathleen Clarke[12]

I was told by an N.C.O. who was on the staff of the jail at that time that Tom Clarke had expressed a wish to see Daly before he (Clarke) was executed. . . .

This N.C.O. told me that when Comdt Daly arrived at Kilmainham with his escort he was informed that as Tom Clarke was about to be executed he could not see him. Daly said he would like to see him dead or alive and he was allowed to remain. When the three men were executed their bodies lay in an old shed in which prisoners broke stones in bad weather. He then took off his cap, knelt down and prayed for some time. He put on his cap, saluted again and returned to his escort. Daly stood in the same spot the following morning for his own execution.

—Michael Soughly, constable in the Dublin Metropolitan Police, witness statement[13]

At 2:00 am all visitors to the prison, without exception, were ordered to leave. Just after 3:30 in the morning on May 3, the three men were taken separately to the execution yard and shot by firing squad. The firing party was drawn from the 59th Division and commanded by Major C. Harold Heathcote. The official reports stated that all three men met their fate bravely.

Kathleen Clarke's personal trauma was not over with the execution of her husband. Neither was that of Mrs. Margaret Pearse, mother of Pádraig and Willie. Later that same day more courts-martial were held, twenty-two in all, with more guilty verdicts. Twenty prisoners received death sentences. Maxwell commuted sixteen of these. He upheld four. The four to be shot were Ned Daly, Kathleen Clarke's brother; Willie Pearse; Michael O'Hanrahan, who had been second-in-command to MacDonagh at Jacob's Biscuit Factory; and Joseph Mary Plunkett, one of the signatories of the Proclamation of the Irish Republic. Scant evidence was given against either O'Hanrahan or Willie Pearse, who, apart from being Pádraig Pearse's brother, was a relatively insignificant figure in the Rising. That evening the four men were taken to Kilmainham and told that they would be shot the next morning. Kathleen Clarke had been allowed to go home, having visited her husband the previous night before his execution at dawn. She now made her way back to Kilmainham to visit her brother. The events of

top: Illustrated portrait of Tom Clarke. He was executed on May 3.

bottom: The first edition of the *Irish Independent* to be published after the Rising.

I had sent the children down to Limerick and there was no-one in the house. I don't drink but I had whiskey and brandy in the house in case any wounded were brought in. Now, I thought, I'll have one twenty four hours of oblivion; and I took out a bottle of port and filled myself out a glass. I thought it would be strong. But I was awake again in an hour. My sister came up from the country and that night a lorry came and took us to Kilmainham to say goodbye to my brother. I heard it coming before any of them and I said, 'it's coming to take us to Ned. He's going to be shot.' They thought I was going off my head. But a few minutes later we all heard it. Then it stopped outside the house. My sister didn't want me to go but I insisted. My brother was in uniform. He looked about eighteen. There was a group of officers outside the cell. They seemed to have some spite against him. The soldier holding the candle had been in my husband's firing party. He said that my husband was the bravest man he's seen. I lost the baby about a week later. I don't know if it was a boy or a girl.

—Kathleen Clarke[14]

the night were particularly poignant. Plunkett, who was seriously ill from tuberculosis, requested and was granted permission to marry his fiancée, Grace Gifford. The marriage took place at midnight in his cell, with two soldiers holding rifles as witnesses, before he was taken out to be shot. (Grace Gifford's sister, Muriel, had been married to Thomas MacDonagh.) Plunkett's father, Count Plunkett, a prominent nationalist, had been arrested after the Rising and was being held in Richmond Barracks. He managed to catch a glimpse of his son at a distance just after his court-martial. It would be the last time he would see him.

Illustrated portrait of Edward (Ned) Daly.
He was executed on May 4.

All four were shot in the morning. Maxwell was now walking a tightrope, under pressure not to overreact but also adamant that the guilty needed to be punished. Later that day, Plunkett's two brothers were court-martialed and sentenced to death. Maxwell commuted their sentences to ten years penal servitude. The courts-martial continued on relentlessly.

The only woman to be court-martialed was Countess Markievicz. Seventy-five women in total had been arrested after the Easter Rising. Maxwell dismissed most of them as "silly little girls," releasing sixty-eight under caution, but others, "the more prominent and dangerous ones," including Countess Plunkett, Joseph Mary Plunkett's mother, were detained in Kilmainham Gaol, where

left: Illustrated portrait of Joseph Mary Plunkett. He was executed on May 4.

right: Grace Gifford, married to Joseph Mary Plunkett in Kilmainham Gaol shortly before his execution.

FOUR MORE REBEL LEADERS SHOT
RESIGNATION OF MR. BIRRELL

THE INSURRECTION ENDED.

FOUR MORE DEATH SENTENCES

18 REBELS SENT TO PENAL SERVITUDE

THE CITY RETURNING TO NORMAL CONDITIONS.

CLEARING THE STREETS OF THE DEBRIS

FURTHER CAPTURES OF PRISONERS: MANY STRIKING INCIDENTS.

WEDDING OF A DOOMED LEADER

Four more of the arrested rebel leaders suffered the death penalty after conviction by court martial, viz., Joseph Plunkett, Edward Daly, Michael O'Hanrahan and Wm. Pearse.

In addition, 18 other insurgents were sentenced to death, but had their sentences commuted to penal servitude, 17 to 10 years', and one to 8. Further trials are proceeding.

Total Shot to Date - - - - - 7
Total sent to Penal Servitude - - 18

A MERCHANT'S ORDEAL.

DOOMED LEADER'S WEDDING.

A PATHETIC INCIDENT.

OFFICIAL.
4 MORE LEADERS SHOT.

EIGHTEEN OTHER REBELS SENTENCED TO PENAL SERVITUDE.

The following further results of the trials of rebels are announced:—

Conviction and Death Sentence.

JOSEPH PLUNKETT.   MICHAEL O'HANRAHAN.
EDWARD DALY.   WILLIAM PEARSE.

Penal Servitude.

10 YEARS.

Thomas Bevan.   Patrick M'Nestry.   James Melins.
Thomas Walsh.   Peter Clancy.   J. J. Reid.
Finian Lynch.   William Tobin.   John Williams.
Michael Mervyn.   George Irvine.   Francis Fahy.
Denis O'Callaghan.   John Doherty.   Richard Davys.
P. E. Sweeney.   J. J. Walsh.

5 YEARS.

John M'Garry.

Further trials are proceeding.

NEW BATCH OF INCIDENTS

MORE PRISONERS TAKEN

STRIKING EPISODES OF THE RISING

ADDITIONAL COURTMARTIAL TRIALS.
NEW CHIEF AND UNDER SECRETARIES.

FURTHER SENTENCES ON INSURGENTS.

MAJOR M'BRIDE SHOT.

THE KING'S MESSAGE TO TROOPS AND POLICE FORCES.

ANOTHER 1,000 PRISONERS DEPORTED.

VIVID STORY OF THE FIVE HOURS' DEADLY BATTLE AT ASHBOURNE.

NEW CHIEF AND UNDER SECRETARIES.

Major John M'Bride was executed by sentence of courtmartial yesterday. Thomas Hunter and William Cosgrave, T.C., had their death sentences commuted to penal servitude for life, and three others—Edward Duggan, Pierce Beasley, and Joseph Maguinness—were each sentenced to 3 years' penal servitude.

Total executed to date 8
Total sent to penal servitude 28

  2 For life,   1 For 3 years, and
 17 For 10 years,   3 For 3 years.

LIST OF THE DEAD.

ANOTHER REBEL LEADER SHOT

MAJOR McBRIDE PAYS DEATH PENALTY

TWO GET LIFE SENTENCES, AND THREE 3 YEARS' PENAL SERVITUDE.

OFFICIAL.

5th May, 1916.

Trials by court-martial of rebels proceeded 5th May, 1916. Confirmation has only taken place in three cases, namely, those of

THOMAS HUNTER.   JOHN McBRIDE.   WILLIAM COSGRAVE.

THE MEN AND WHO THEY ARE.

THE EXECUTED.

LIFE SENTENCES.

TEN YEARS' SENTENCES.

THE CAPTURED INSURGENTS.

MORE RISING INCIDENTS.

MARTIAL LAW AND ITS EFFECTS

MILITARY SEARCH FOR FUGITIVES.

VARIED EXPERIENCES.

---

top: *Irish Independent*, May 5.

bottom: *Irish Independent*, May 6.

opposite-top: Major John McBride, formerly married to Maud Gonne. He was executed on May 5.

opposite-bottom: Michael O'Hanrahan, second-in-command to Thomas MacDonagh at Jacob's Biscuit Factory. He was executed on May 4.

they heard the executions from their cells. Countess Markievicz was treated differently. She attracted a particular level of antagonism due, in the main, to her Ascendancy background. Many of her peers saw her as a despicable traitor to her class.

Although Maxwell himself felt she was "bloodguilty and dangerous," her death sentence was confirmed but immediately commuted to one of penal servitude for life, "solely and only on account of her sex." It had been made clear to Maxwell that Prime Minister Asquith and the cabinet wouldn't countenance executing a woman. (The Germans had executed Edith Cavell, a nurse whom they accused of being a spy, and received much opprobrium as a result.)

On the morning of Low Sunday, we heard of the surrender and then no news whatever until the following Wednesday, 3 May, when at about ten a.m. the Reverend Father Aloysius arrived to break the terrible news that Pat had made the supreme sacrifice—that he had died that morning at a quarter to four. . . .

Towards midnight we were aroused from an attempt to get a few hours sleep by the arrival of a military lorry. I went to the hall door and was given a note saying that the prisoner, William Pearse, desired to see us. I returned to the bedroom and said to Mother, "More bad news. Willie wants to see us as he is going too." . . .

We talked quietly and calmly and chiefly about personal matters. We told him how proud we were of him and Pat and that we were satisfied they had done right . . . we bade a last good-bye and left him gazing after us, one longing, sad look, till the cell door closed. . . .

Though our sorrow and loss are very great indeed, we were resigned. Pat and Willie, so wonderfully united in life, were also united in death.

—Margaret Pearse, sister of Pádraig and Willie[15]

The Tide Begins to Turn

By now both Augustine Birrell and Sir Matthew Nathan had resigned and left Ireland for good. Maxwell had been clear as to his policy in dealing with the rebels, and for the moment the government backed him. By Monday morning, May 8, one week after the surrender of rebel forces, twelve men had been executed. The country was under martial law. Over 3,500 people, more than double the number who had taken part in the Rising, had been arrested, even in areas that had seen no activity. A substantial number of those not court-martialed were deported to internment camps and prisons in England.

It is clear that there were differing opinions regarding the Rising since the surrender. The newspapers were vitriolic in their condemnation. The *Irish Times*, the main unionist newspaper, and the *Irish Independent*, owned by William Martin Murphy, Connolly's sworn enemy, and representing Catholic business interests and mainstream nationalism, were relentless in criticizing the actions of the rebels. But public opinion was beginning to shift. The initial reaction of many people in Ireland to the Rising, at best lukewarm and ambivalent, at worst hostile, was now giving way to a grudging respect that was growing with each execution and

Windsor Castle
TO: General Sir John Maxwell, G.O.C. in Chief, Irish Command, Dublin
Now that the recent lamentable outbreak has finally been quelled I wish to express to my gallant troops in Ireland, to the Royal Irish Constabulary and to the Dublin Metropolitan Police my deep sense of the wholehearted devotion to duty and spirit of self-sacrifice with which throughout they have acted.
George R.I.

—Telegram sent to Maxwell by George V, May 4, 1916

left: Seán Heuston, who was executed on May 8. Kingsbridge was later renamed Heuston Station in his honor.

above: Con Colbert, a teacher at St Enda's, executed on May 8 for his part in the Rising.

with the mass arrests and daily deportations. Most importantly, given the Great War, the British were anxiously watching the reaction across the Atlantic in America.

The events in Ireland had been closely followed in the American press since Casement's highly publicized arrest on Good Friday. The *New York Times* devoted front-page attention to the events in Ireland for fourteen straight days, from April 25 to May 8. On April 29, the day Pearse surrendered, the *New York Times* had eight articles on page one and eight more on page two. It also carried an editorial and commentary column in-

side. Initially the coverage was hostile to the rebels, portraying them as irresponsible and as pawns of the Germans, but later articles would be more positive about the Rising and its leaders.

Anxious to retain and to further strengthen American support for their war effort, the British were worried about opinion in the United States becoming sympathetic to the rebels in Ireland. The British ambassador was Sir Cecil Spring Rice, who came from an Irish Ascendancy family. Ironically, he was a cousin of Mary Spring Rice, an ardent Irish nationalist and separatist who had organized the Howth gunrunning, bringing in on the *Asgard*

left: Illustrated portrait of Michael Mallin. He was executed on May 8.

right: Michael Mallin's widow, Agnes, and their five children.

nine hundred German Mauser rifles, most of which had been used in the Rising.

The ambassador's main objective was to change the American policy of neutrality in the war, and he was anxious that nothing should inflame U.S. opinion against Britain. Maxwell's strat-

A military officer came to us in the hold of the boat and inquired as to what we wanted. Tom Hunter told him very quickly that we wanted tea, sugar and cigarettes. He left and returned with a good supply. He then asked several questions and summed up by saying that he was at the Battle of Mons and that it was only "so and so" to the battle in O'Connell St, but that we the Volunteers must have known that he was an Irishman and although he had not even a stick of rhubarb with which to defend himself he did not even get hit. He further remarked that we had started the "racket" too soon. And he bid us goodnight and good luck and the boat steamed off.

The portholes were our only means of observation and when passing Lambay Island and Ireland's Eye, Séamus Hughes gave us the "Last Glimpse of Erin" in his usual great style.

—Peadar Doyle, describing the prisoners' deportation from North Wall to prisons in Britain, witness statement[16]

Though the last glimpse of Erin with
   sorrow I see,
Yet wherever thou art shall seem Erin
   to me;
In exile thy bosom shall still be my
   home,
And thine eyes make my climate
   wherever we roam.

To the gloom of some desert or cold
   rocky shore,
Where the eye of the stranger can
   haunt us no more,
I will fly with my Coulin, and think the
   rough wind
Less rude than the foes we leave
   frowning behind.

And I'll gaze on thy gold hair as
   graceful it wreathes,
And hang o'er thy soft harp as wildly
   it breathes;
Nor dread that the cold hearted
   Saxon will tear
One chord from that harp, or one
   lock from that hair.

—sung by Irish Volunteer
   Séamus Hughes, a member of the
   Jacob's Biscuit Factory garrison,
   on board a prison ship following
   his deportation after the Rising[17]

Illustrated portrait of Éamonn Ceannt.
He was executed on May 8.

egy in Ireland was doing little to help him. Mass protests were organized in cities with large Irish populations, such as New York, San Francisco, and Boston. Hundreds flocked to join the Friends of Irish Freedom, a new Irish American republican organization, founded in March 1916, that brought together many Irish American groups under one banner. The growing hostility to Britain and support and sympathy for the rebels began to be reflected in the newspapers. By May 4 articles were appearing in the *New York Times* that used the term "martyrs" to describe Pearse and the other executed leaders. On May 7, Joyce Kilmer, the well-known poet and a recent convert to Catholicism, wrote an article with the headline "Poets March in Van of Irish Revolt." This new designation of the Rising as the poets' rebellion would be highly significant in changing public perception of the event.

The change in public opinion was not confined to Ireland and the United States alone. One of Britain's stated reasons for going to war with Germany had been its opposition to what it portrayed as German, or Prussian, militarism. To some in Britain, the response to the Rising—martial law, secret courts-martial, executions—was perilously close to what they were supposed to be fighting.

On May 9, the death sentence of Éamon de Valera, the commandant of Boland's Mill, handed down by court-martial, came before Maxwell. He was finding himself under increasing political pressure from Asquith to execute only known

9th May
In view of the gravity of the rebellion and its connection with German intrigue and propaganda and, in view of the great loss of life and destruction of property resulting therefrom, the General Officer Commanding-in-Chief [Maxwell] has found it imperative to inflict the most severe sentences on the known organizers of this detestable rising and on those commanders who took an active part in the actual fighting which occurred. It is hoped that these examples will be sufficient to act as a deterrent to intriguers and to bring home to them that the murder of his Majesty's liege subjects, or other acts calculated to imperil the safety of the Realm will not be tolerated.
—Official government statement[18]

The attitude of public opinion as to the Irish rebellion, is on the whole satisfactory. The press seems to be agreed that the movement is suicidal and in the interests of Germany alone. The attitude of the majority of Irish is uncertain, but if the movement spreads the effect here will be very serious indeed. All are agreed that it will be dangerous to make Casement a martyr.
—Report from Ambassador Sir Cecil Spring Rice to Sir Edward Grey, British Foreign Secretary, April 28, 1916

The leaders of the revolutionary forces were almost without exception men of literary tastes and training, who went into battle, as one of the dispatches phrased it, with a revolver in one hand and a copy of Sophocles in the other.
—Joyce Kilmer, *New York Times* Sunday Magazine, May 7, 1916

ringleaders. The crown prosecutor for the courts-martial, Lt. William Wylie, recounted that Maxwell showed him a telegraph from Asquith to this effect. Maxwell asked Wylie who was next on the list to be tried. "Somebody called de Valera, Sir," he replied. Maxwell was not familiar with him and asked Wylie whether he considered him someone that would make trouble in the future. Wylie replied that he didn't think so, that de Valera was not one of the leaders and was unimportant. Maxwell commuted his sentence. It would be a serious error of judgment. Among those others whose death sentences had been commuted and who would play significant roles were W. T. Cosgrave, first President of the Irish Free State, and Thomas Ashe, who would die on a hunger strike a year later.

But not all sentences were reduced. In the early hours of May 9, another execution took place, this time in Cork Detention Center. The execution of Thomas Kent followed a series of events earlier at his County Cork farmhouse.

Arrest of two Kent brothers in County Cork. Thomas Kent was executed on May 9.

In line with Maxwell's policy, a raiding party had come to arrest the Kent brothers near Fermoy after the Rising. They were prominent separatists, or Sinn Féiners, as the rebels and their sympathizers were now being called. A gun battle ensued, resulting in the deaths of two of the brothers and a policeman, Constable Rowe of the RIC. Two of the brothers were arrested. Thomas was sentenced to death at his court-martial, whereas his brother William was granted a reprieve. On the same day that Thomas Kent faced the firing squad in Cork, the last two signatories of the Proclamation, Seán Mac Diarmada and James Connolly, were court-martialed in Dublin.

The executions had a profound effect on public opinion, and not only in nationalist Ireland. Prominent public figures such as George Bernard Shaw fulminated against the executions in the London *Daily News*. Even among mainstream moderate nationalists, attitudes were changing. On the day of the first executions, of Pearse, Clarke, and MacDonagh, John Redmond had spoken against the Rising in the House of Commons and blamed Germany. Ten days later, following twelve executions and growing outrage at home in Ireland, John Dillon, a senior figure in Redmond's Irish Party, made a speech that shocked and provoked outrage among his listeners in the House of Commons. The target of his anger was the British government and its policy of retribution.

My own view is that the men who were shot in cold blood, after their capture or surrender, were prisoners of war, and that it was, therefore, entirely incorrect to slaughter them. The relation of Ireland to Dublin Castle is, in this respect, precisely that of the Balkan States to Turkey, of Belgium or the city of Lille to the Kaiser, and of the United States to Great Britain.

. . . It is absolutely impossible to slaughter a man in this position without making him a martyr and a hero, even though the day before the rising he may have been only a minor poet. The shot Irishmen will now take their places beside Emmet and the Manchester Martyrs in Ireland. And beside the heroes of Poland and Serbia and Belgium in Europe; and nothing in Heaven or earth can prevent it. . . . The Military authorities and the English Government must have known that they were canonizing their prisoners. . . .

I remain an Irishman and am bound to contradict any implication that I can regard as a traitor any Irishman taken in a fight for Irish independence against the British government, which was a fair fight in everything, except the enormous odds my countrymen had to face.

—George Bernard Shaw,
Daily News, London,
May 10, 1916

This attempted deadly blow at Home Rule is made more wicked and more insolent by the fact that Germany plotted it, Germany organized it, and Germany paid for it.

—John Redmond
in the House of Commons,
May 2, 1916[19]

You are letting loose a river of blood. . . . It is the first rebellion that ever took place in Ireland where you had the majority on your side. It is the fruit of our life work . . . and now you are washing away our whole life work in a sea of blood.

What is poisoning the mind of Ireland, and rapidly poisoning it, is the secrecy of these trials and the continuance of these executions.

It is not murderers who are being executed; it is insurgents who have fought a clean fight, a brave fight, however misguided, and it would be a damned good thing for you, if your soldiers were able to put up as good a fight as those men in Dublin— three thousand men against twenty thousand with machine guns and artillery.

—John Dillon
in the House of Commons,
May 11, 1916

A Policy of Vengeance?

Two of the most important leaders, the last remaining signatories of the Proclamation, remained in custody, still under sentence of death. Egged on by a hostile Dublin press, Asquith would show them no mercy. At 3:00 am on May 12, a prison chaplain heard the last confession of Seán Mac Diarmada. Fifteen minutes before he was taken out to the yard to be shot, he wrote his last words. In the early hours of that same morning, James Connolly, still suffering badly from his wounds, was brought to Kilmainham Gaol by military ambulance. He had just received his last

> There are two other persons who are under sentence of death—a sentence which has been confirmed by the General, both of whom signed the Proclamation and took an active part ... in these two cases the extreme penalty must be paid.
>
> —Asquith in the House of Commons, May 11, 1916

left: Illustrated portrait of Seán Mac Diarmada. He was executed on May 12.

above: The last letter of Seán Mac Diarmada, written shortly before his execution.

visit from his family. Major Heathcote was once again the officer-in-command of the firing squad. Connolly, unable to stand, was brought in on a stretcher and placed on a kitchen chair to be shot. When asked by the priest attending him whether he forgave those who were to shoot him, he replied, "I do, Father, I respect every brave man who does his duty."

The executions of Mac Diarmada and Connolly added to the growing anger in America. Spring Rice wrote in a memo that "the Irish here . . . have blood in their eyes when they look our way." Mass meetings continued in American cities. On May 14, two days after Connolly's execution, five thousand people packed into Carnegie Hall in New York to protest events in Ireland. An estimated twenty thousand others congregated outside in the street, unable to get in.

General Maxwell had, early in the process, already decided that all of those executed would be buried in quicklime graves without a coffin. He had refused to allow the bodies of the executed leaders to be buried by their families, to prevent their graves becoming martyrs' shrines.

The *New York Times*, front page, Saturday, May 13, announcing the executions of John McDermott (Seán Mac Diarmada) and James Connolly.

The first time I saw him was in the afternoon, and he was just in a little room, we went up the stairs, up the staircase and turned to the right, to a little room off that, there were soldiers all the way up the stairs . . . two soldiers were at the door. Mama, my mother was with me, when we went in to the room, there was an officer in uniform, but he was a medical officer. Before we went in we were told we weren't to give him any news or talk about what happened, we were only to give him personal news, so of course we said alright. I think some bits of news had slipped through to him the way things do. He was concerned with leaving us, what would happen to a family of mainly girls and mother. That there'd be no life for us at all, he wanted us to go to the States. He had some writings, he wanted me to get in touch with Sheehy Skeffington, get him to arrange it. That was the last straw, I tried to keep to the rules until then. I said, Skeffington is gone, and he said 'what' and I said 'yes', in Portobello barracks and that's all I said for fear I might be put out of the room.

—Nora (Connolly) O'Brien,
eldest daughter of
James Connolly [20]

The next time I saw him was about one o'clock at night, and the message that was given was that the prisoner James Connolly wanted to see his wife and eldest daughter. All had been executed up to that point except for him and Sean McDermott [Seán Mac Diarmada] and it immediately jumped to my mind that he was going to be executed, but Mama had the idea that he wasn't well. We got ready and were taken in an army lorry, right through Dublin, and it was an eerie journey, [in] O'Connell Street you could still smell the burning, and no one [was] on the streets, because there was a curfew in place at that time. We went through the dimly lit streets and not a soul [was] on the streets, we didn't even see a soldier until we came to the bridge. We went up to the castle, everytime we went there we were searched to make sure we didn't bring anything with us to help him end his life I suppose.

When we got in to my Father he said 'Well Lily, I suppose you know what this means?', 'Oh no, not that', 'yes Lily,' she broke down and she said 'such a beautiful life James', 'a beautiful life Lily', he said, 'wasn't it a full life Lily and isn't this a good end. Look Lily please don't cry, you'll unman me'. She tried to control herself and I was trying to control myself too. Then he said to me put

your hand down on the bed, that's a copy of my statement to the court martial, try to get it out, so I took it. We talked about things, he was trying to plan our life after he was gone.

Then they told us time was up and we had to go and he was to be shot at dawn, we couldn't get Mama away from the bed and a nurse had to come to help her away. I went to the door and then I went back to him, that was the last I saw of him. We went back in the morning to claim his body but of course they wouldn't hear of it. Mama had asked the nurse who was helping her from the room 'get me a lock of his hair' and she did, she posted it afterwards.

I couldn't understand how they could execute him as he was lying there helpless, and I asked Fr. Aloysius who was with him, how they did it, he said they took him from the stretcher, down to the ambulance and the ambulance took him to Kilmainham gaol and they tied him to a chair, before he died I asked him to say a prayer for the men who were about to shoot him, and he said 'I'll say a prayer for all brave men who do their duty.' One of the firing squad came to my mother afterwards and told her he was one of the firing squad, and he couldn't go on living without my mother's forgiveness. 'It's a

terrible thing, I'm a Welshman and in the labour movement all my life, and to think I should send a bullet in to that man.' Mama said 'Don't worry, you only did your duty' and he [James Connolly] said a prayer for all men who did their duty.

—Nora (Connolly) O'Brien [21]

_____

I, Sean Mac Diarmada, before paying the penalty of death for my love of country and hatred of her slavery, desire to leave this message to my fellow countrymen:

That I die as I lived, bearing no malice to any man, and in perfect peace with Almighty God. The principles for which I give my life are so sacred that I now walk to my death in the most perfectly calm and collected manner.

I go to my death for Ireland's cause as fearlessly as I worked for that sacred cause during all my short life.

I ask the reverend Eugene McCarthy, who has prepared me to meet my God, and who has given me courage to undergo this ordeal, to convey this message to my fellow-countrymen. God Save Ireland.

—Seán Mac Diarmada,
written fifteen minutes before his
execution on May 12 [22]

ʒo Saoraiʋ ʋia éiʀe.

✠

ANNIVERSARY
MASSES,

APRIL and MAY, 1917.

———

Mother Eire, weep not for them,
Raise your head beside your Cross.
Such Deaths would sanctify the Nation,
Such Deaths are glorious gains not loss.
—L. ní ḃ.

a Ʋia ʒléʒil na péile aʒuʀ a
Ataiʀ na nʒʀáʀ,
Le ʋo naoṁtoil ʋo céaʀaʋ aʒuʀ
ʋo ḃʀataʋ ċun ḃáiʀ,
a ʋonṁic, ʋo ḟaoʀ ʀinn ó'n
ḃpeacaʋ ʀa ṗáiʀ,
Réiʋtiʒ na ʒaeʋil ḃoċta aʒuʀ
leaʀuiʒ ʒan ʀpáʀ.

Picture postcards of the executed rebels were displayed in almost every shop window, and their faces were gazed upon with silent veneration by the passers-by.... Up and down Sackville Street urchins ran selling broad sheets purporting to contain 'The last and inspiring speech of Thomas MacDonagh'.... So far as one can tell, except among the shop-keepers who had not received compensation for their losses and among the upper classes, all resentment against the Sinn Feiners had died away.

—Douglas Goldring, writer,
on a visit to Dublin,
end of May 1916[23]

Maxwell was right to be worried. In the event, graves were not necessary. Memory cards, postcards, pamphlets, poems, songs, and memorabilia were widely distributed in the following weeks and months, contributing to the canonization of the executed leaders and their cause.

The aftermath of the executions saw a process of beatification of the executed leaders in which the role of the Catholic Church was significant. Requiem masses were held, in which the piety and purity of the dead leaders were emphasized. The *Catholic Bulletin* published a major series of articles, "Events of Easter Week," which were hugely influential. Moreover, the mythologizing and iconography of the idea of "blood sacrifice" (*dulci et decorum est pro patria mori*; "it is sweet and proper to die for one's country"), widespread in Europe generally in the years both preceding and during the Great War, now took on a particularly Irish and Gaelic hue.

left: His Easter Offering: Angel, Erin, Soldier, and Irish Flag. A typical poster drawing on Catholic and Celtic iconography, 1917.

center: Mass Card for Anniversary Masses, 1917.

Easter Week Memorial Poster, 1917.

Irish sentimentality will turn these graves into martyrs' shrines; annual processions would be made to them, which will cause constant irritation in this country.

—Letter from Maxwell to Maurice Bonham Carter, Asquith's private secretary, May 1916[24]

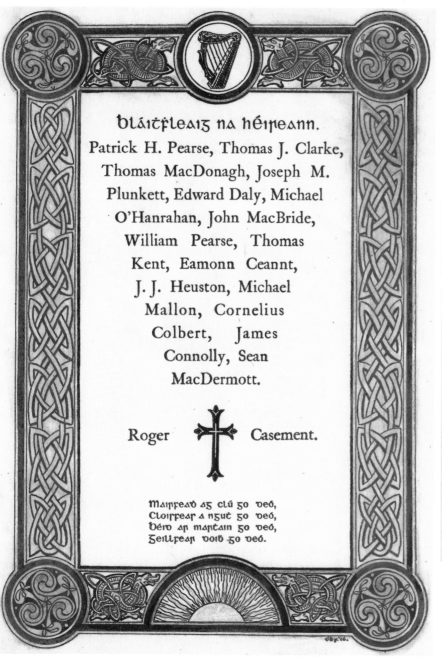

blátfleaᴢ na héipeann.

Patrick H. Pearse, Thomas J. Clarke,
Thomas MacDonagh, Joseph M.
Plunkett, Edward Daly, Michael
O'Hanrahan, John MacBride,
William Pearse, Thomas
Kent, Eamonn Ceannt,
J. J. Heuston, Michael
Mallon, Cornelius
Colbert, James
Connolly, Sean
MacDermott.

Roger ☨ Casement.

Maiᴘfeaᴅ aᴢ clú ᴢo ᴅeó,
Cloiᴘfeaᴘ a nᴣuᴅ ᴢo ᴅeó,
béiᴅ aᴘ maᴘᴅain ᴢo ᴅeó,
ᴣeillfeaᴘ ᴅoiᴅ ᴢo ᴅeó.

In Loving Memory

OF

Pádraiᴄ MacPiarais
(PATRICK HENRY PEARSE)

Who gave his life for Ireland

On May 3rd, 1916

Aged 36 Years.

ALSO HIS BELOVED AND DEVOTED BROTHER

William MacPiarais
(WILLIAM JAMES PEARSE)

Who gave his life in the same holy cause

On May 4th, 1916

Aged 34 Years.

ᴣo nᴅéanaiᴅ ᴅia ᴛᴘócaiᴘe aᴘ a
n-anamnaiᴅ.

GENTLEST HEART OF JESUS, ever
present in the Blessed Sacrament, ever con-
sumed with burning love for the poor captive souls
in Purgatory, have mercy on the souls of Thy
servants, PATRICK and WILLIAM; bring them from
the shadows of exile to the bright home of Heaven,
where, we trust, Thou and Thy Blessed Mother
have woven for them a crown of unfading bliss.
Amen.

A MOTHER SPEAKS

Dear Mary, that didst see thy first born Son
Go forth to die amid the scorn of men
For whom He died,
Receive my two dear sons into thy arms
Who also have gone out to die for men,
And keep them by thee till I come to them.
Dear Mary, I have shared thy sorrow,
And soon shall share thy joy.

The red-gold flame of Erin's name
Confronts the world once more;
So Irishmen, remember then.
And raise your hearts with pride,
For great men, and straight men,
Have fought for you and died.

left: Memorial leaflet for the executed leaders.

center: Mass card for the Pearse brothers.

right: Memorial card for Thomas MacDonagh.

Irish nationalist opinion, buoyed by huge support from the Irish diaspora, had swung behind the rebels and their now-martyred leaders. The British had sown dragons' teeth that very soon would come back to bite them. Attempts were made to stem the flow of nationalist sympathy for the rebels. Under the widespread powers given by the Defence of the Realm Act, the press censor's office now swung into action and tried to stop American reports being republished in Irish newspapers. A painting by Walter Paget of "the GPO just before its evacuation" was banned "on the grounds that it was inexpedient."

Fifteen executions had taken place. Other death sentences had been commuted to various terms of imprisonment in the light of growing

Easter Week by Walter Paget, originally banned by press censor's office.

protest at home and abroad. One prominent rebel leader remained, however. Roger Casement had been in custody in England since his arrest on Good Friday. As a knight of the realm who had conspired with Germany during wartime, he would be tried for high treason. Because of his celebrity, his trial attracted enormous public interest not only in Ireland but also in Britain and most especially in the United States. Controversial diaries, which clearly indicated his homosexuality, were used shamelessly to ruin his reputation. They were circulated in order to weaken support for a possible reprieve. The press, notably the *Daily Express*, undertook a campaign of vilification. Internationally there were widespread calls for clemency. In the United States, the Senate passed two resolutions to ask President Wilson to intercede. Sympathy for the Irish rebels was at its height.

High Treason, a painting by Sir John Lavery depicting Sir Robert Casement's trial for treason.

Despite the repeated warnings of Ambassador Spring Rice in Washington about the probable impact of Casement's execution, the cabinet refused to budge. Roger Casement was hanged in Pentonville Prison on August 3, 1916.

While opinion in nationalist Ireland was beginning to turn towards the rebels, attitudes among Ulster unionists were clear and unyielding: the rebels were traitors, guilty of a stab in the back during a time of war. If the Easter Rising of 1916 came to signify Irish republicans' ultimate sacrifice for freedom, the Battle of the Somme in June would give Ulster unionists their own date of blood sacrifice for king and empire.

The Rising prompted a cultural response as well as a political one. The writings of the 1916 leaders attracted a new readership. Editions of the poems of Pearse, Plunkett, and MacDonagh were published in late 1916 and in 1917. W. B. Yeats, who had known many of the leaders personally, published his poetic response.

> As to the poor fellows who have given themselves for Ireland, no one will venture to question the purity and nobility of their motives or the splendor of their courage. But many blame them for attempting a hopeless enterprise. Yet one cannot help noticing that since Easter Monday Home Rule has come with a bound into the sphere of practical politics.
> —Dr. Dwyer, Bishop of Limerick, in a letter of June 2, 1916, to the Limerick Board of Guardians [26]

left: Casement leaving court in London after his trial. He was hanged in Pentonville Prison on August 3.

right: The *Daily Express*, Thursday, August 3, describing Casement's last hours. He was hanged that morning despite last-minute appeals for clemency.

Easter week and its sequel occupy the minds of us all. . . . History does not record a cleaner fight than that fought by the Volunteers. Another landmark has been fixed in the course of our history. Another epoch has opened. Whatever the future has in store, no-one who knows anything of the country can fail to see that the founts of our nationalism have been stirred to their depths, that there has been a great searching of hearts and a great quickening of religious feeling. It looks as if with the Requiem Masses for the dead, there is united, as if by common consent, a general union of prayer for Ireland amounting almost to exaltation.

—*Catholic Bulletin*,
July 1916

Sixteen Dead Men

O but we talked at large before
The sixteen men were shot,
But who can talk of give and take,
What should be and what not
While those dead men are loitering
    there
To stir the boiling pot?

You say that we should still the land
Till Germany's overcome;
But who is there to argue that
Now Pearse is deaf and dumb?
And is there logic to outweigh
MacDonagh's bony thumb?

How could you dream they'd listen
That have an ear alone
For those new comrades they have
    found,
Lord Edward and Wolfe Tone,
Or meddle with our give and take
That converse bone to bone?

—W. B. Yeats[27]

Salutation

*Written for those who took part in the
1916 Rebellion*

Your dream had left me numb and cold
But yet my spirit rose in pride,
Re-fashioning in burnished gold
The images of those who died,
Or were shut in the penal cell—
Here's to you, Pearse, your dream,
    not mine,
But yet the thought—for this you
    fell—
Turns all life's water into wine.
I listened to high talk from you,
Thomas MacDonagh, and it seemed
The words were idle, but they grew
To nobleness, by death redeemed.
Life cannot utter things more great
Than life can meet with sacrifice,
High words were equalled by high fate,
You paid the price. You paid the price.

The hope lives on, age after age,
Earth with her beauty might be won
For labour as a heritage—
For this has Ireland lost a son,
This hope into a flame to fan
Men have put life by with a smile.
Here's to you Connolly, my man,
Who cast the last torch on the pile.

Here's to the women of our race
Stood by them in the fiery hour
Rapt, lest some weakness in their
    blood
Rob manhood of a single power—
You, brave as such a hope forlorn,
Who smiled through crack of shot and
    shell,
Though the world look on you with
    scorn,
Here's to you Constance in your cell.

Here's to you, men I never met,
But hope to meet behind the veil,
Thronged on some starry parapet
That looks down upon Inisfail,
And see the confluence of dreams
That clashed together in our night,
One river born of many streams
Roll in one blaze of blinding light.

—George William Russell (A.E.)[28]

"All changed . . ."

By 1917 it was clear that the rebellion, while ostensibly a failure, was creating the conditions for a national revolution that would change the course of Irish history. Political support swung firmly behind Sinn Féin. But it was a newly revitalized and much more radicalized party than it had been before the Rising, as was the general populace to whom it looked for support. By the end of the year, the British decided to release most of the remaining prisoners from jails and internment camps. The changed mood of the people could be seen clearly by the huge crowds that turned out to welcome them. These returning prisoners threw themselves into organizing Sinn Féin and the Irish Volunteers. They included Éamon de Valera, Countess Markievicz, and Michael Collins.

Frongoch internment camp, North Wales, 1916/1917.

Further proof of the profound change in the mood of the country came in the spring of 1917, when a by-election, to fill a vacant seat in the House of Commons, was held in North Roscommon. The Sinn Féin candidate was Count Plunkett, father of Joseph Mary Plunkett. The link with 1916 was explicit. Other by-elections followed, with some of the newly released prisoners standing as Sinn Féin candidates. Among the successful candidates was de Valera, who was elected for Clare. Support for Sinn Féin continued to grow, as did the reformed and reorganized Volunteers. The first anniversary of the Rising was marked by demonstrations proclaiming, "The Irish Republic Lives!"

The republicans would soon have another name to add to the list of their martyred dead. Thomas Ashe had been a rebel in 1916 and was a leader in one of the few successful military actions of the week, which had taken place in Ashbourne, County Meath. Ashe had his death sentence commuted and was imprisoned until the general release. Already an iconic figure, he had

Irish prisoners in Stafford jail in England, 1916/1917. Fifth from the right is Michael Collins. These prisoners, on their release, would constitute a new revolutionary leadership.

been re-arrested for making a seditious speech. He refused to be treated as a criminal and went on a hunger strike. On September 25, 1917, he died in Mountjoy Jail in Dublin while being force-fed. His funeral would galvanize many in Ireland and further increase political support for Sinn Féin.

The changed times were seen clearly in the General Election of 1918. Support for the Irish Party collapsed and Sinn Féin scored a remarkable victory. This would lead to the establishment of an abstentionist parliament, Dáil Éireann, which would seek to make the Proclamation of 1916 a reality. Many of those appointed ministers of the new republican government were veterans of the Rising: Éamon de Valera became president, Countess Markievicz was minister for labor, W. T. Cosgrave was minister for local government, and Michael Collins was minister for finance in their new republic. Collins, who had been a relatively junior figure in the GPO garrison during the Rising, was growing in prominence. He believed Britain would not give Ireland her freedom without a fight.

Countess Markievicz greeted by cheering crowds following her release.

opposite: Rebuilding Liberty Hall, 1917.

The volley of shots at the funeral of Thomas Ashe, 1917.

Éamon de Valera addresses a crowd in County Clare while campaigning for Sinn Féin in 1917.

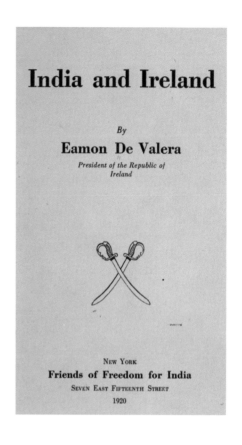

India and Ireland

By
Eamon De Valera

President of the Republic of Ireland

NEW YORK
Friends of Freedom for India
SEVEN EAST FIFTEENTH STREET
1920

Collins was highly critical of the way the Rising had been organized. When the Irish Volunteers, now titled the Irish Republican Army, the IRA, next took on the British in arms, it had none of the chivalry associated with the Easter Rising. Collins had learned a bitter but important lesson. The next blow would be struck by means of a guerilla campaign in the countryside and by a series of assassinations in the cities. The decade following the Rising was turbulent, witnessing a guerrilla war between the British and the IRA.

While Michael Collins and the IRA conducted the war at home in Ireland, de Valera spent most of the war of independence in the United States successfully drumming up both financial and moral support from Irish America. Collins's ruthless tactics forced the British to call a truce. The treaty that followed was deeply divisive. Those on the republican side, including de Valera, Mrs. Pearse, Kathleen Clarke, and many relatives of the executed leaders, denounced the terms as a sell-out of the ideals of the Easter Rising. Others, includ-

left: The First Dáil (Dáil Éireann) meet at Dublin's Mansion House, January 21, 1919.

right: Cover of pamphlet written by Éamon de Valera.

ing Collins and Cosgrave, took a more pragmatic view. Although the treaty was ratified, its opponents refused to accept it.

A bitter civil war ensued, one that saw men and women who had been comrades in 1916 take opposite sides. It would also see the death of Michael Collins, killed in an ambush by his erstwhile comrades-in-arms. The victory of the pro-treaty government forces cemented the existence of two states on the island. One was called Northern Ireland, set up in 1920, with six northeastern counties still part of the United Kingdom. The other was an independent Irish state, known as the Irish Free State, comprising the remaining twenty-six counties, which in 1949 would be proclaimed the Republic of Ireland and would claim 1916 as its founding event.

The effect of 1916 would not only be felt in Ireland. Its ideals would influence the burgeoning anti-imperialist and anticolonial movements from India to Vietnam to the former colonial states in Africa. It would have a particular resonance for Bengali revolutionaries and other militant Indian nationalists. Bengali radicals staged an armed rebellion in 1930 in the city of Chittagong in what is now Bangladesh, then a part of British India. This revolt, known as the Chittagong Uprising, took place on Easter, 1930, and directly echoed the earlier events in Dublin. The leader of this rising, Surya Sen, was a devotee of Pearse and the other Irish republican leaders. He was later captured and hanged by the British. Lenin also acknowledged the significance of the Rising. Although he felt that the Irish had risen too soon, he believed the Rising in Ireland was "one hundred times more powerful a blow against the British Empire than one in Africa or Asia."

The memory of 1916 did survive, as Pearse and the other leaders predicted at the time, and influenced future generations in Ireland and further afield. It struck the first blow in a struggle that would eventually put an end to the age of empire. The sun would set for the British Empire, first in Ireland, then India, then Asia, then its territories in Africa. The map of the world would be profoundly different. All changed, changed utterly.

EASTER, 1916

Bewildered them till they died?
I write it out in a verse—
MacDonagh and MacBride
And Connolly and Pearse
Now and in time to be,
Wherever green is worn,
Are changed, changed utterly:
A terrible beauty is born.

W. B. YEATS.

Sept. 25, 1916.

W. B. Yeats, "Easter, 1916," excerpt, from one of the twenty-five copies of the poem privately printed and circulated in 1917, before its first publication in 1920.

Acknowledgments

THIS BOOK GREW OUT OF A PROJECT INITIATED BY THE KEOUGH-Naughton Institute for Irish Studies at the University of Notre Dame to mark the centenary of the Easter Rising in Dublin in 1916. Without the incredible on-going support of the institute and its fellows and staff, in particular, Director Christopher Fox, Beth Bland, Mary Hendriksen, and Margaret Lloyd, this book, and the documentary series to which it is an accompanying volume, would have remained a pipe dream.

I thank Mary McAleese for generously agreeing to write the foreword to this book. I also thank her and Martin McAleese for stimulating and inspiring conversations.

I would like to acknowledge the vital role of Vanessa Gildea, who undertook most of the photographic research.

I also want to recognize the help and support of Peter McQuillan, chair of the Department of Irish Language and Literature, and all of my colleagues in IRLL; Jim Collins, chair of the Department of Film, Theatre, and Television, and all of my colleagues in FTT; Dean John McGreevy and the faculty of the College of Arts and Letters; Dean Scott Appleby and the Keough School of Global Affairs; Kevin Whelan, Eimear Clowry Delaney, and the team at O'Connell House, Dublin; and everyone at the University of Notre Dame who assisted with the project, including Paul Browne, Tim Flanagan, Lou Nanni, Rudi Reyes, and Ken Garcia. I would also like to acknowledge the overwhelming generosity of our donors, who make our work possible.

I would also like to thank the wonderful scholars who shared their insights with me during long fruitful discussions and interviews both on and off camera. They include Gearóid Ó Tuathaigh, Tom Bartlett, Declan Kiberd, Joe Lee, Mary Daly, Ronan Fanning, Kevin Whelan, Patrick Griffin, Alvin Jackson, Robert Schmuhl, Margaret O'Callaghan, Mike Cronin, Ruán O'Donnell, John Kelly, Malcolm Sen, Ashis Nandy, Jim Smyth, Diarmaid Ferriter, Caitríona Crowe, Senia Paseta, Joanna Innes, Fearghal McGarry, Keith Jeffery, Charles Townshend, Roy Foster, Kate O'Malley, David Fitzpatrick, William Mulligan, Anne Dolan, and Owen Dudley Edwards, among others.

My thanks also to the following: Linda Cullen, Stuart Switzer, Jackie Larkin, Angela Delaney, Mary Flanagan, Kate Hayes, and all at Coco Television, as well as Ruán Magan, Pat Collins, Paul Rankin, Aoife Carey, Judy Fox, Dympna Fogarty, the Fogarty family, Mary Houlihan, Barbara Corcoran, Mary Elizabeth and Declan Burke Kennedy, and all our hugely supportive friends and neighbors in Carrigahorig.

I want to pay special tribute to the wonderful editorial and design team at the University of Notre Dame Press, in particular to Rebecca DeBoer, Matthew Dowd, Wendy McMillen, and the director of the press, Steve Wrinn.

Finally, my deepest gratitude, as always, to my family: my mother Mary, Joan and George B., Martina and George N., Tim, John and Eileen, Shauna and Cora, and especially Gaye, whose love and support sustains me always.

Notes

BMH Bureau of Military History, Military Archives, Ireland

BPMA British Postal Museum and Archive

CO Colonial Office National Archives, Kew

IWM Imperial War Museum

NLI National Library of Ireland

NMI National Museum of Ireland

PRO Public Records Office, National Archives, London

RTÉ Raidió Teilifís Éireann

WO War Office, PRO

WS Witness Statement

PART 1. AWAKENING

1. This poem was first published in the United States in *McClure's* magazine and newspapers including *The New York Sun*, February 5, 1899, during America's colonization of the Philippines. Kipling had originally written it for Victoria's diamond jubilee.

2. Maud Gonne's article was published on April 4, 1900, in *The United Irishman*, edited by Arthur Griffith. The newspaper's office was raided in an attempt to seize the offending edition.

3. Hyde's lecture was delivered to the Irish National Literary Society in Dublin, November 25, 1892, and later published in pamphlet form.

4. Milligan's poem "When I Was a Little Girl" was first published in a collection edited by George Russell (A.E.), entitled *Hero Lays* (Dublin: Maunsell & Co., 1908).

5. This English-language version of "La Carmagnole" is taken from the singing of Frank Harte and Karen Casey.

6. The ballad "The Bold Fenian Men" was written by Michael Scanlon and has been recorded by many Irish artists.

7. The song "Skibbereen" was first published in *The Irish Singer's Own Book* (Boston: Thomas B. Noonan, 1880), attributed to Patrick Carpenter, a native of Skibbereen in County Cork. It was recorded by the collector John Avery Lomax in the 1930s from Irish immigrants in Michigan.

8. NLI MS 108, John Devoy Papers.

9. Kathleen Clarke, *Revolutionary Woman: Kathleen Clarke, 1878–1972; An Autobiography*, ed. Helen Litton (Dublin: O'Brien Press, 1991), 35.

10. The ballad "God Save Ireland" was written by T. D. Sullivan in 1867. It was recorded in 1906 and popularized in the U.S. by tenor John McCormack. It was the unofficial anthem of Irish nationalism for many years.

11. WS 391, BMH. Helena Moloney was then editor of *Bean na hÉireann*.

12. CO 904/27, p. 43.

13. Kipling's poem was first published in the London *Morning Post*, April 9, 1912.

14. Clarke, quoted in Sean Cronin, *The McGarrity Papers* (Tralee, Ireland: Anvil Books, 1972), 37–38.

15. Published in Padraic Pearse, *Political Writings and Speeches*, ed. Desmond Ryan (Dublin: Phoenix Press, reprint ed., 1966).

16. Ibid.

17. Crawford, quoted in R. F. Foster, *Modern Ireland* (London: Penguin, 1990), 470.

18. See *Churchill: The Power of Words*, ed. Martin Gilbert (Boston: Da Capo Press, 2013), 84–85.

19. Quoted in his memoir: Viscount Grey of Fallodon, *Twenty-Five Years, 1892–1916* (New York: Frederick A. Stokes, 1925), 2:20.

20. Griffith's article was published in *Sinn Féin*; original in NLI.

21. J. L. Stewart-Moore, "Random Recollections," IWM 77/39/1.

PART 2. INSURRECTION

1. University College Dublin archives. Also available at Trinity Letters Project online. Letter no. 2. http://dh.tcd.ie/letters1916/.

2. WS 391, BMH.

3. WS 286, BMH.

4. Margaret Skinnider, *Doing My Bit for Ireland* (New York: The Century Co., 1917), 90–91.

5. "The Dublin Brigade," quoted in Charles Townshend, *Easter 1916: The Irish Rebellion* (London: Penguin, 2006), 152.

6. WS 1604, BMH.

7. Countess Markievicz, "Women in the Fight," in *Dublin 1916*, ed. Roger McHugh (London: Arlington Books, 1966),122.

8. Skinnider, *Doing My Bit for Ireland*, 92, 95.

9. W. J. Brennan-Whitmore, *Dublin Burning: The Easter Rising from Behind the Barricades* (Dublin: Gill & Macmillan, 2013), 46.

10. Skinnider, *Doing My Bit for Ireland*, 95–97.

11. NLI MS 49,809/2. The letter was written on May 2 but deals with earlier events.

12. WS 391, BMH.

13. Royal Commission on the Rebellion in Ireland: Minutes of Evidence CMD 8279. Ref. no. HO 45/10810/312350, National Archives, Kew.

14. WS 687, BMH.

15. Arthur Hamilton Norway, "Irish Experiences in War," in *The Sinn Féin Rebellion as They Saw It*, ed. Keith Jeffery (Dublin: Irish Academic Press, 1999), 109–11.

16. BPMA Post 31/80b, Guthrie to Kenny in his report of May 6, 1916, quoted in Stephen Ferguson, *Business as Usual: GPO Staff in 1916* (Cork: Mercier Press, 2012), 42–43, 46.

17. Skinnider, *Doing My Bit for Ireland*, 106, 109, 110, 111.

18. Mary Louisa Hamilton Norway, *The Sinn Fein Rebellion as I Saw It* (originally published London: Smith, Elder, 1916), reprinted in *The Sinn Féin Rebellion as They Saw It*, ed. Keith Jeffery, 35, 37. All page numbers for *The Sinn Fein Rebellion as I Saw It* are from the Jeffery collection.

19. WS 242, BMH.

20. Ernie O'Malley, *On Another Man's Wound* (originally published London, 1936; repr. Cork: Mercier Press, 2013), 20–22.

21. Garland's letter to his father was originally published in the *Auckland Star*, June 1916. Available digitally from National Library of New Zealand. Garland was a medical orderly from the hospital ship *Marama*. Despite his noncombatant status, he took an active part in the fighting throughout the week. For a fuller account, see Hugh Keane, "New Zealanders in the 1916 Irish Rebellion," in *Volunteer*, vol. 40 (July 2014): 44–52.

22. Mary Hamilton Norway, *The Sinn Fein Rebellion as I Saw It*, 39.

23. Countess Markievicz, "Women in the Fight," in *Dublin 1916*, ed. McHugh.

24. Skinnider, *Doing My Bit for Ireland*, 113–15.

25. One of the Garrison, "Inside Trinity College," originally published *Blackwood's Magazine*, July 1916; reprinted in *Dublin 1916*, ed. McHugh, 160–61.

26. Garland, letter to his father, *Auckland Star*, June 1916. A small number of members of the Anzacs (Australian and New Zealand Army Corps) and other dominion forces in the British Army were in Dublin for convalescence and holiday leave from service in World War I. They were caught up in the rebellion, and some made their way to Trinity College to volunteer in its defense.

27. WS 391, BMH.

28. WS 391, BMH.

29. Mary Hamilton Norway, *The Sinn Fein Rebellion as I Saw It*, 40–41.

30. Ibid., 41.

31. Humphries, quoted in Michael T. Foy and Brian Barton, *The Easter Rising* (originally published Stroud: Sutton Publishing, 1999; later edition, Stroud: The History Press, 2011), 179. Page numbers are from the 2011 edition.

32. "Reflections on Easter Week 1916," Trinity College Dublin Archives, IE TCD MS 10343/6.

33. One of the Garrison, "Inside Trinity College," in *Dublin 1916*, ed. McHugh, 162–63.

34. Skinnider, *Doing My Bit for Ireland*, 119–20, 123–24.

35. Garland, letter to his father, *Auckland Star*, June 1916.

36. One of the Garrison, "Inside Trinity College," in *Dublin 1916*, ed. McHugh, 161–62. The dead man was twenty-year-old Gerald Keogh of the Irish Volunteers, from Cullenswood, Ranelagh, in Dublin. He had been a pupil of Pearse's at St Enda's. Three of his brothers were also active in the Rising. He had been sent by Pearse as a dispatch rider to St Stephens Green and was killed on his way back to the GPO. For a fuller account of Keogh, see Raymond Keogh, "'Well dressed and from a respectable street,'" in *History Ireland* (March/April 2009).

37. From an article by Hartnell first published in the women's magazine *The Lady of the House*, 1916, quoted in chapter 9 of Alex Findlater, *Findlaters: The Story of a Dublin Merchant Family*, Pearse Street Library Archive REF338.7/FIN. Published Dublin: A. & A. Farmar, 2001.

38. Mary Hamilton Norway, *The Sinn Fein Rebellion as I Saw It*, 52.

39. RTÉ archive 11 DO1345.

40. WS 208, BMH.

41. The first paragraph is from Skinnider, *Doing My Bit for Ireland*, 134, 137; the second from an audio recording of Margaret Skinnider, RTÉ archive; the rest from *Doing My Bit for Ireland*, 146, 147–48.

42. Ryan, quoted in Foy and Barton, *The Easter Rising*, 185.

43. One of the Garrison, "Inside Trinity College," in *Dublin 1916*, ed. McHugh, 166.

44. O'Malley, *On Another Man's Wound*.

45. PRO, WO 35 67.

46. WS 687, BMH.

47. One of the Garrison, "Inside Trinity College," in *Dublin 1916*, ed. McHugh, 167–68.

48. National Archives, Kew, London British Parliamentary Papers.

49. James Stephens, *The Insurrection in Dublin: An Eyewitness Account of the Easter Rising, 1916* (originally published in 1916; repr. New York: Barnes & Noble, 1999), 57.

50. Dick Humphries, "Easter Week," NLI MS 22725.

51. Staines, quoted in Foy and Barton, *The Easter Rising*, 190. See also WS 284, BMH.

52. Quoted in Richard Killeen, *A Short History of the 1916 Rising* (Dublin: Gill & Macmillan, 2009), 89–92.

53. Quoted in ibid., 94, 96.

54. Maxwell Papers, Princeton University Library.

55. Stephens, *The Insurrection in Dublin*, 65.

56. NLI MS 49,809/1.

57. WS 687, BMH.

58. The O'Rahilly wrote this note on the back of a letter from his son that he had received while he was in the GPO.

59. Quotations of Captain De Courcy-Wheeler, based on his diary, are found in chapter 9 of *Findlaters: The Story of a Dublin Merchant Family*.

60. Quoted in Brian Barton, *The Secret Court Martial Records of the Easter Rising* (Stroud: The History Press, 2010), 57. Original in Kilmainham Museum.

61. Original in NMI.

62. Quoted in Barton, *The Secret Court Martial Records of the Easter Rising*, 57. Original in Kilmainham Museum.

63. *Findlaters: The Story of a Dublin Merchant Family*, chap. 9.

64. NLI MS 15,453.

65. Quoted in Barton, *The Secret Court Martial Records of the Easter Rising*, 337.

66. RTÉ LX4652.

67. *Findlaters: The Story of a Dublin Merchant Family*, chap. 9.

68. Account by Nurse Elizabeth O'Farrell, "The Surrender," *The Capuchin Annual* (1917).

69. Mary Hamilton Norway, *The Sinn Fein Rebellion as I Saw It*, 63–64.

70. *Findlaters: The Story of a Dublin Merchant Family*, chap. 9.

71. NLI, De Courcy-Wheeler papers.

72. WS 920, BMH.

PART 3. WHEN MYTH AND HISTORY RHYME

1. Mary Hamilton Norway, *The Sinn Fein Rebellion as I Saw It*, 64.

2. PRO.

3. Pradaic Pearse, *The Letters of P. H. Pearse*, ed. Séamus Ó Buachalla (Atlantic Highlands, NJ: Humanities Press, 1980), 74–75.

4. PRO, WO 35/67/2, quoted in Barton, *The Secret Court Martial Records of the Easter Rising*, 79.

5. *The Letters of P. H. Pearse*, 86.

6. PRO, WO 71/345, quoted in Barton, *The Secret Court Martial Records of the Easter Rising*, 130–31.

7. Quoted in Barton, *The Secret Court Martial Records of the Easter Rising*, 123.

8. *The Letters of P. H. Pearse.*

9. PRO, WO 71/346, quoted in Barton, *The Secret Court Martial Records of the Easter Rising*, 144–45.

10. In Piaras F. Mac Lochlainn, ed., *Last Words: Letters and Statements of the Leaders Executed after the Rising at Easter 1916* (Dublin: Stationery Office, 1990).

11. PRO, WO 71/347, quoted in Barton, *The Secret Court Martial Records of the Easter Rising*, 159.

12. A more detailed account may be found in Clarke, *Revolutionary Woman: Kathleen Clarke, 1878–1972*, 92–96.

13. WS 189, BMH.

14. A more detailed account may be found in Clarke, *Revolutionary Woman: Kathleen Clarke, 1878–1972*, 117–18, 127.

15. Margaret Pearse, "'Patrick and Willie Pearse," *The Capuchin Annual* (1943), 86–93.

16. WS 155, BMH.

17. See Thomas Moore, *Irish Melodies*, vol. 1.

18. PRO.

19. Hansard, for quotations from the House of Commons.

20. RTÉ interview of Nora Connolly, 1965. See also WS 286, BMH.

21. RTÉ interview of Nora Connolly, 1965. See also WS 286, BMH; NLI MS 13947.

22. Quoted in Gerard MacAtasney, *Sean MacDiarmada: The Mind of a Revolution* (Manorhamilton, Co. Leitrum: Drumlin Publications, 2004).

23. Goldring, quoted in Clair Wills, *Dublin 1916: The Siege of the GPO* (London: Profile Books, 2009), 105–6.

24. University College Dublin in P150/512, partially quoted in Barton, *The Secret Court Martial Records of the Easter Rising*, 81.

25. Quoted in Angus Mitchell, *Roger Casement* (Dublin: O'Brien Press, 2013).

26. Dwyer, quoted in John H. H. Whyte, "1916—Revolution and Religion," in *Leaders and Men of the Easter Rising: Dublin 1916*, ed. F. X. Martin (Ithaca, NY: Cornell University Press, 1967), 331.

27. In *Collected Poems of W. B. Yeats*, A New Edition, ed. Richard J. Finneran (New York: Macmillan, 1989), and numerous other collections.

28. See "Seven Poems," in *Dublin 1916*, ed. McHugh.

29. De Valera, quoted in Townshend, *Easter 1916: The Irish Rebellion*, 331.

30. In Lenin, *Collected Works*, vol. 22 (Moscow, 1964).

Credits

All images are courtesy of the respective source. Images are listed by page number and caption.

ABBREVIATIONS

BMH Bureau of Military History, Military Archives, Ireland
GAA Gaelic Athletic Association
IWM Imperial War Museum
KGA Kilmainham Gaol Museum Archive
LOC Library of Congress
NLI National Library of Ireland
NMI National Museum of Ireland
RTÉ Raidió Teilifís Éireann

FRONTMATTER

iii Behind Wynn's Hotel, Lower Abbey Street.

iv Rubble.

vi *Church Street Barricades, 1916*, painting by Joseph McGill. Hyde Collection, Áras an Uachtaráin.

viii Sackville Street before the Rising. Reproduced from the original held by the Department of Special Collections of the Hesburgh Libraries of the University of Notre Dame.

x View of Dublin buildings. BMH.

PART ONE. AWAKENING

Dublin, June 11, 2011

3   President Mary McAleese with Queen Elizabeth at the Garden of Remembrance, Dublin, June 11, 2011. © RTÉ
           Stills Library.

Dublin, July 8, 1911

4   Crowds line the streets at College Green, Dublin, 1911, to greet the newly crowned King George V. © RTÉ Stills
           Library.

4   Programme of the Royal Progress. Reproduced courtesy of NLI.

5   King George V, 1911. Wikimedia Commons.

The Age of Empire

7   Map showing British Empire, 1886. Wikimedia Commons.

8   Queen Victoria. Wikimedia Commons.

9   Queen Victoria's jubilee procession in London, 1897. Wikimedia Commons.

"That Most Distressful Country"

10   Maps showing Ireland before and after the plantations of the sixteenth and seventeenth centuries. Wikimedia
           Commons.

11   Sir Henry Sidney, Lord Deputy of Ireland under Elizabeth I, setting out from Dublin Castle. (Detail from a plate
           in *The Image of Irelande* by John Derrick, 1581.) Trinity College, Dublin.

11   English depiction of severed heads of Irish rebels, 1608. Trinity College, Dublin.

12   Artist's impression of Dublin Castle, bulwark of English rule in Ireland. Wikimedia Commons.

13   Queen Victoria visiting Dublin, 1900. Reproduced courtesy of NLI.

13   A young Maud Gonne. Wikimedia Commons.

14   Boer fighters, 1900. At Spion Kop. Project Gutenberg.

15   Munster Fusiliers during the Boer War. Royal Munster Fusiliers Association.

16   Major John McBride. Reproduced courtesy of NLI.

17   Boer women and children in a concentration camp. Wikimedia Commons.

New Beginnings

18   A young Douglas Hyde. Wikimedia Commons.

19   Lady Gregory. Abbey Theatre Archives.

19   Joseph Mary Plunkett. NMI.

19   William Butler Yeats. LOC.

19   Pádraig Pearse. Wikimedia Commons.

20   Program for the first inter-county competition under GAA rules, held at the estate of Charles Stewart Parnell, October 31, 1886. GAA Museum, Croke Park, Dublin.

21   GAA teams, late 1800s. GAA Museum, Croke Park, Dublin.

22   Arthur Griffith addressing a crowd in Dublin. Wikimedia Commons.

22   James Connolly. NMI.

22   Thomas MacDonagh. NMI.

22   Helena Moloney. NMI.

22   Countess Markievicz. Wikimedia Commons.

22   Alice Milligan. Reproduced courtesy of NLI.

23   Members of the Irish Socialist Republican Party with James Connolly (front center with moustache), 1901. From Donal Nevin, *James Connolly: "A Full Life."*

23   Membership card for the London Branch of Conradh na Gaeilge, 1901. Reproduced courtesy of NLI.

24   The first edition of the *Shan Van Vocht*, published in Belfast, January 15, 1896. Villanova University.

24   Order form for *Bean na hÉireann*. Reproduced courtesy of NLI.

25   Front page of *Bean na hÉireann*, April 1909. Reproduced courtesy of NLI.

25   Page from *Bean na hÉireann* showing an advertisement for Pearse's school, St Enda's. Reproduced courtesy of NLI.

25   Nationalist Women's Association flyer. Reproduced courtesy of NLI.

26   Façade of the old Abbey Theatre, 1913. Abbey Theatre Archives.

26   Playbill for the Irish National Theatre Society at the Abbey Theatre, 1905. Reproduced courtesy of NLI.

26   *Kathleen Ni Houlihan*, Abbey stage, 1902, with Maud Gonne (far right) in leading role. Abbey Theatre Archives.

27   Con Colbert conducting drill with boys in St Enda's. Reproduced courtesy of NLI.

27   Willie and Pádraig Pearse. Photo by Hedge, 1914. St Enda's Museum.

28–29   Éamonn Ceannt, adjudicator (front center, slightly to the right, with moustache), with pipers at the Oireachtas, Rotunda, Dublin, ca. 1900. Allen Library, Dublin.

30   Robert Emmet. Reproduced courtesy of NLI.

30   Patriots of 1798. Reproduced courtesy of NLI.

31   Depiction of French Revolution by Eugene Delacroix, *La liberté guidant le peuple*. Wikimedia Commons.

31   Wolfe Tone pleads Ireland's case with Napoleon. Reproduced courtesy of NLI.

33   The Fenian Banner, 1866. LOC.

The American Connection

34   Irish immigrants in the U.S., 1909. Wikimedia Commons.

35   Immigrants arrive at Ellis Island, New York, 1902. Wikimedia Commons.

36   John Devoy. LOC.

36   Chaplain and men of the Irish Brigade during the American Civil War. Wikimedia Commons.

37   Fenian poster. LOC.

37   Depiction of the Fenian ship *Erin's Hope*. Wikimedia Commons.

38   Tom Clarke in 1883. Reproduced courtesy of NLI.

38   Jeremiah O'Donovan Rossa. Reproduced courtesy of NLI.

39   Kathleen Clarke. Burns Library, Boston College.

39   Seán Mac Diarmada. Reproduced courtesy of NLI.

The Daughters of Ireland and Mother India

40   Madan Lal Dhingra.

41   A poster commemorating the Manchester Martyrs, William Allen, Michael Larkin, and Michael O'Brien, executed November 23, 1867. Wikimedia Commons.

"We'll Keep the Red Flag Flying"

44   Handbill advertising "the Irish American Orator" James Connolly, 1910. Reproduced courtesy of NLI.

45   James Connolly addressing a May Day rally in New York City, 1908. LOC.

The "Irish Question"

46   John Redmond, the hero of Home Rule. Muriels Stills.

47   Charles Stewart Parnell. Wikimedia Commons.

The Unionist Response

48   Sir Edward Carson putting the first signature to the Ulster Covenant, City Hall, Belfast, September 28, 1912. James Craig stands to his left. Ulster Museum, National Museums Northern Ireland.

49   Carson inspecting members of the Ulster Volunteer Force. Reproduced courtesy of NLI.

51   Carson addressing an anti–Home Rule rally. LOC.

51   Anti–Home Rule postcard representing "Donegall Place, Belfast, under Home Rule." Reproduced courtesy of NLI.

51   "Stand Back Redmond" anti–Home Rule postcard.

The Response of Nationalism

53   Eoin MacNeill. Reproduced courtesy of NLI.

53   Bulmer Hobson. Reproduced courtesy of NLI.

53   Young members of Na Fianna Éireann, 1914. Reproduced courtesy of NLI.

53   Report of the founding of the Irish Volunteers, *Irish Times*, November 26, 1913. Reproduced courtesy of NLI.

54   Group of slaves in the Belgian Congo, 1905. From *La Tragedia del Congo*, by Sir Roger Casement et al.

54   Roger Casement. NMI.

55   Group photograph of Cumann na mBan. KGA.

56   *Irish Independent*, September 1, 1913. Reproduced courtesy of NLI.

57   Baton charge by police during the Dublin Lockout of 1913. © RTÉ Stills Library.

58   Image of the presentation to Countess Markievicz from the Irish Transport and General Workers Union for her services during the 1913 Lockout. Reproduced courtesy of NLI.

59   Advertisement in the *Gaelic American*, February 28, 1914, p. 8. Reproduced courtesy of NLI.

War Clouds Gather

60   Unloading arms from the *Asgard* at Howth pier. Trinity College, Dublin.

61   Report in the *Irish Independent* on the aftermath of the Bachelor's Walk killings of civilians. Reproduced courtesy of NLI.

62   Funeral cortege for the victims of Bachelor's Walk passes by the GPO.

63   John Redmond and members of the National Volunteers. Reproduced courtesy of NLI.

The Great War

64   The *Irish Independent* announces England's declaration of war against Germany. Reproduced courtesy of NLI.

65   Irish infantrymen off to World War I, 1915. IWM.

66   Pearse (to the right of priest) waits to give the oration at the graveside of O'Donovan Rossa. James Langton.

66   Funeral procession program for Jeremiah O'Donovan Rossa. Reproduced courtesy of NLI.

68–69   Members of the ICA parade outside Croydon Park, Dublin, 1915. KGA.

70   Roger Casement and John Devoy in the U.S. before Casement's departure for Germany. Villanova University.

71   The *Aud*, which carried German arms for the Rising. Mercier Press Archive.

Holy Thursday, April 20

72   Casement on the U-19 submarine setting off for Ireland. He had shaved his beard in an effort to remain incognito. Mercier Press Archive.

Good Friday, April 21

74   Report of Casement's capture in the *Ulster Herald*. Reproduced courtesy of NLI.

Easter Saturday, April 22

75   *Sunday Independent*, Easter Sunday, April 23, 1916, carrying MacNeill's countermand and reporting on events in Kerry.

76   Volunteers marching before the Rising. Reproduced courtesy of NLI.

Easter Sunday, April 23

78   Letter from Eoin MacNeill to Éamon de Valera, Easter Sunday, 1916. Trinity Letters Project online.

79   Augustine Birrell. University of Glasgow Archives.

79   Sir Matthew Nathan. National Portrait Gallery.

80   The Vice-Regal Lodge in the Phoenix Park, Dublin, home to the Viceroy, Lord Wimborne, and his family. Reproduced courtesy of NLI.

81   The Viceroy, Lord Wimborne. Reproduced courtesy of NLI.

Easter Monday, April 24

82   Liberty Hall before the Rising. Reproduced courtesy of NLI.

83   The General Post Office (GPO) and Sackville Street just before the Rising. An Post Archives.

84   Thomas Clarke. Getty images.

84   Edward (Ned) Daly. NMI.

84   Margaret Skinnider. Frontispiece of her *Doing My Bit for Ireland*. Reproduced from the original held by the Department of Special Collections of the Hesburgh Libraries of the University of Notre Dame.

84   Éamon de Valera in Volunteer uniform, 1916. James Langton.

84   Countess Markievicz in ICA uniform. BMH.

84   Seán Connolly. Reproduced courtesy of NLI.

84   Michael Mallin. Lorcan Collins.

84   Éamonn Ceannt. Mary Evans.

85   Rebels inside the GPO. BMH.

87   Dublin Castle gate, ca. 1916. City Hall is on the left. Reproduced courtesy of NLI.

87   The yard at Dublin Castle. Reproduced courtesy of NLI.

87   City Hall. Seán Connolly was shot dead on the roof on Monday afternoon. Reproduced courtesy of NLI.

88   Sergeant James O'Brien, the first fatality of the Rising. KGA.

90   Illustration of Jacob's Biscuit Factory, ca. 1916, garrisoned by Volunteers under the command of Thomas MacDonagh.

90   St Stephen's Green seen from the Shelbourne Hotel. Reproduced courtesy of NLI.

91   Boland's Mill, garrisoned by Volunteers under the command of Éamon de Valera. Reproduced courtesy of NLI.

92   The Four Courts, garrisoned by Volunteers under the command of Edward (Ned) Daly. Reproduced courtesy of NLI.

93   The Proclamation of the Irish Republic as read by Pádraig Pearse outside the GPO, Easter Monday. Reproduced courtesy of NLI.

93   Painting of Pádraig Pearse as president of the Irish Republic, by Leo Whelan. Mercier Press Archive.

96   South Dublin Union, garrisoned by Volunteers under the command of Éamonn Ceannt.

96   Trinity College from Dame Street. Reproduced courtesy of NLI.

98   British Lancers pass a dead horse in Dublin city center. James Langton.

100   John Joly. Trinity College, Dublin.

102   Kingsbridge Station. Reproduced courtesy of NLI.

103   Brigadier General Lowe. Reproduced courtesy of NLI.

Tuesday, April 25

105   Dependents of Irish soldiers in British Army, waiting for allowances. British Postal Museum.

Wednesday, April 26

108   Front page of the London *Daily Express* on Wednesday, April 26. UK Press Online.

109   Members of the Sherwood Foresters on Northumberland Road. University College, Dublin, de Valera papers.

109   Michael Malone. Reproduced courtesy of NLI.

110   Mount Street Bridge and Clanwilliam House after the final assault. NMI.

112   The British gunboat *Helga*. Allen Library, Dublin.

113   Liberty Hall following the shelling by the *Helga*. Reproduced from the original held by the Department of Special Collections of the Hesburgh Libraries of the University of Notre Dame.

114   Francis Sheehy Skeffington. Reproduced from the original held by the Department of Special Collections of the Hesburgh Libraries of the University of Notre Dame.

114   Captain J. C. Bowen-Colthurst.

118–19   British troops in Trinity College. Mercier Press Archive.

Thursday, April 27

120   Burning buildings in Sackville Street. Getty images.

120   Winifred Kearney. KGA.

121   British troops in military truck. NMI.

122   Irish Volunteers inside the GPO. Reproduced courtesy of NLI.

122   British soldiers at barricade. Camera Press.

Friday, April 28

124   General Sir John Maxwell. Princeton University.

126   The O'Rahilly in full Volunteer uniform, ca. 1915. University College, Dublin, Humphreys Archive.

126   The O'Rahilly and his wife, Nancy, ca. 1912. University College, Dublin, Humphreys Archive.

Saturday, April 29

128   Elizabeth O'Farrell in her nurse's uniform. Glasnevin Museum.

129   Pádraig Pearse surrenders to General Lowe. Nurse Elizabeth O'Farrell is standing out of sight to the right of Pearse. NMI.

132   James Connolly lies on a stretcher following the surrender. Mick O'Farrell.

133   Rebel soldier marched over O'Connell Bridge. IWM.

Sunday, April 30

134   Committal shots of Countess Markievicz taken after her arrest. Clare Museum.

134   Michael Mallin and Countess Markievicz after their surrender. © RTÉ Stills Library.

136   Fr. Augustine Hayden, OFM Cap. Capuchin Archives.

137   Fr. Aloysius Travers, OFM Cap. Capuchin Archives.

Monday, May 1

PART THREE. WHEN MYTH AND HISTORY RHYME

Aftermath

Paying the Price: Courts-Martial and Executions

155   Major John McBride, formerly married to Maud Gonne. He was executed on May 5. TopFoto (UK).

155   Michael O'Hanrahan, second-in-command to Thomas MacDonagh at Jacob's Biscuit Factory. He was executed on May 4. Reproduced courtesy of NLI.

The Tide Begins to Turn

156   Seán Heuston, who was executed on May 8. Kingsbridge was later renamed Heuston Station in his honor. Reproduced courtesy of NLI.

156   Con Colbert, a teacher at St Enda's, executed on May 8 for his part in the Rising. Reproduced courtesy of NLI.

157   Illustrated portrait of Michael Mallin. He was executed on May 8. NMI.

157   Michael Mallin's widow, Agnes, and their five children. KGA.

158   Illustrated portrait of Éamonn Ceannt. He was executed on May 8. NMI.

160   Arrest of two Kent brothers in County Cork. Thomas Kent was executed on May 9. Reproduced courtesy of NLI.

A Policy of Vengeance?

162   Illustrated portrait of Seán Mac Diarmada. He was executed on May 12. NMI.

162   The last letter of Seán Mac Diarmada, written shortly before his execution.

163   The *New York Times*, front page, Saturday, May 13, announcing the executions of John McDermott (Seán Mac Diarmada) and James Connolly.

165   His Easter Offering: Angel, Erin, Soldier, and Irish Flag. A typical poster drawing on Catholic and Celtic iconography, 1917. Reproduced courtesy of NLI.

165   Mass Card for Anniversary Masses, 1917. Reproduced courtesy of NLI.

166   Easter Week Memorial Poster, 1917. Reproduced courtesy of NLI.

167   Memorial leaflet for the executed leaders. Allen Library, Dublin.

167   Mass card for the Pearse brothers.

167   Memorial card for Thomas MacDonagh. Reproduced courtesy of NLI.

168   *Easter Week* by Walter Paget, originally banned by press censor's office. Reproduced courtesy of NLI.

169   *High Treason*, a painting by Sir John Lavery depicting Sir Robert Casement's trial for treason. King's Inns, Dublin.

170   Casement leaving court in London after his trial. He was hanged in Pentonville Prison on August 3. NMI.

170   The *Daily Express*, Thursday, August 3, describing Casement's last hours. He was hanged that morning despite last-minute appeals for clemency. UK Press Online.

"All changed . . ."

172   Frongoch internment camp, North Wales, 1916/1917. Reproduced courtesy of NLI.

173   Irish prisoners in Stafford jail in England, 1916/1917. Fifth from the right is Michael Collins. These prisoners, on their release, would constitute a new revolutionary leadership. BMH.

174   Countess Markievicz greeted by cheering crowds following her release. © RTÉ Stills Library.

175   Rebuilding Liberty Hall, 1917. Reproduced courtesy of NLI.

176   The volley of shots at the funeral of Thomas Ashe, 1917.

177   Éamon de Valera addresses a crowd in County Clare while campaigning for Sinn Féin in 1917. Getty images.

178   The First Dáil (Dáil Éireann) meet at Dublin's Mansion House, January 21, 1919. Reproduced courtesy of NLI.

178   Cover of pamphlet written by Éamon de Valera. LOC.

179   W. B. Yeats, "Easter, 1916," excerpt, from one of the twenty-five copies of the poem privately printed and circulated in 1917, before its first publication in 1920. Reproduced from the original held by the Department of Special Collections of the Hesburgh Libraries of the University of Notre Dame.

180   British soldier tends a Trinity College grave, 1916. Reproduced courtesy of NLI.

Index

The letter "f" following a page number denotes an illustration and its caption.

BRÍONA NIC DHIARMADA

is the Thomas J. & Kathleen M. O'Donnell Professor of Irish Studies and concurrent professor of
Film, Television, and Theatre at the University of Notre Dame. She is originator, writer,
and producer of the multipart documentary series, *1916 The Irish Rebellion*.